Self-Care for People with ADHD

100+ Ways to Recharge, De-Stress, and Prioritize You!

Sasha Hamdani, MD

The ADHD Doctor, @thepsychdoctormd

Adams Media

New York   London   Toronto   Sydney   New Delhi

Adams Media
An Imprint of Simon & Schuster, Inc.
100 Technology Center Drive
Stoughton, Massachusetts 02072

Copyright © 2023 by
Simon & Schuster, Inc.

First Adams Media hardcover edition January 2023

ADAMS MEDIA and colophon are trademarks of Simon & Schuster.

For information about special discounts for bulk purchases, please contact Simon & Schuster Special Sales at 1-866-506-1949 or business@simonandschuster.com.

The Simon & Schuster Speakers Bureau can bring authors to your live event. For more information or to book an event contact the Simon & Schuster Speakers Bureau at 1-866-248-3049 or visit our website at www.simonspeakers.com.

Interior design by Julia Jacintho
Interior images © 123RF/Sergey Balakhnichev

Manufactured in the United States of America

5 2023

Library of Congress Cataloging-in-Publication Data has been applied for.

ISBN 978-1-5072-1943-0
ISBN 978-1-5072-1944-7 (ebook)

Dedication

This book was a labor of love and the culmination of many confusing years of navigating through ADHD. I was assured no one reads these, so I can be as nauseatingly earnest as I want:

Thank you for the faith that carried me through dark, weird times and gave me something to hold on to. Thank you to both of my families for being constant supports and especially to my two baby birds for shining so much light into my life. Thank you to my medical school coordinator, Gladys, for hugging me when I needed it most. Thank you to my entire Banner family for gluing back my pieces and making me a physician. Thank you to my social media community for building such a beautiful, inspiring virtual world and allowing me to be my true, authentic self. Thank you to Radhika for being Radhika. And thank you to Leah, who plucked me from obscurity and gave me the golden chance to write this book.

If I think about it too much, I will definitely start crying. So, just thank you from the bottom of my heart.

Contents

Preface

ADHD is a part of me. It is intrinsically woven into my DNA and is expressed in almost every facet of my life. My ADHD has grown with me and changed with new seasons in my life. It has made me realize that caring for myself and my well-being is inherently important and not something that I can push to the side or forget about. ADHD has challenged me but also propelled me to achieve things that I never thought were possible. And it is what led me to write this book.

My symptoms were first noticed in fourth grade in the form of a vivacious little girl who often had difficulty "settling down." Even at that young age, I was acutely aware that I was capable of doing better but just didn't know how. The teacher brought up these concerns to my parents. Days later, I was formally diagnosed with ADHD and started on medication. The difference was immediate. I sailed through school and began to truly enjoy learning. I knew that I wanted to go to medical school, but when I got there, I had to function independently without the support architecture that I had previously known. I felt disillusioned. My entire identity had been defined by academic success and that carefully cultivated image had shattered. It was then that I realized medication on its own wasn't enough.

With a great deal of support, I was able to complete medical school and match into a psychiatry residency. *That* is where my journey changed. For the first time in my life, people *wanted* to talk about what was happening in my brain. In those safe surroundings, I realized that ADHD is not something to be fixed but rather is something to be managed. I had the time and the emotional space to distance myself from the chaos and slowly build organizational structures that suited my brain. I began trying self-care activities to build my focus, calm my emotions, and battle harmful thought patterns. I began to truly embrace my way of thinking differently and saw it for all its positive attributes rather than dwelling on the negative. It felt like a rebirth. With this new reframing and this deeper understanding of my own unique neural network, I felt like I could think more clearly, communicate more effectively, and remain present in the moment.

Since then, I have continued to rely heavily on those life-preserving self-care routines. ADHD doesn't go away, but learning how to capitalize on your strengths and mitigate your weaknesses can help steer your ship to safe harbor. Self-care is not just a series of extravagances; it is also a form of being mindful of your individual needs so you can achieve a healthy, balanced, and happy life. Taking the time and effort toward self-nourishment continues to be the most healing journey of my life.

I am so grateful I was given this opportunity because I was able to write the guide that I wish someone had written for me. Self-care isn't a dazzling epiphany or a single life hack. It is a series of small choices that can lead you to a better you. Let me show you how...

Introduction

Living with attention deficit hyperactivity disorder (ADHD) requires being mindful of things that other people take for granted every day. Tasks and actions that come effortlessly to some people may be difficult for a person with ADHD to achieve. As a result, people with ADHD must learn how to take care of themselves in ways that reward and nourish their brains instead of making them feel like they are being forced to conform through a neurotypical lens. That's why, if you are coexisting with ADHD, it is especially important that you make time to care for yourself.

Developing healthy self-care practices is part of the behavioral management of ADHD. These practices allow you to meet daily life demands, participate more meaningfully, and remain in a healthy mental space. That's where *Self-Care for People with ADHD* comes in. In this book, you will find over one hundred self-care activities that will empower, rejuvenate, and help you be at your best.

Self-care for people living with ADHD involves more than just the stereotypical acts of pampering—it is a cache of survival techniques that prevent you from burning out. These techniques need to be practiced and understood and applied because it takes discipline to take responsibility for your well-being.

Here are just some of the activities you'll find in this book:

- Allow Yourself to De-Mask
- Recognize Your Triggers
- Learn How to Nourish Your Brain
- Understand and Recognize Hyperfocus

- Identify Rejection Sensitivity
- Be Aware of Interrupting
- Push Aside Perfectionism

As a clinician with ADHD, believe me when I tell you that fostering a healthy relationship with your diagnosis is key to living a fulfilling life. People with ADHD are creative, bright, bubbly, and energetic, and they make up a vibrant community that you should take pride in. And if you suspect that you may have ADHD and find yourself saying, "Hey, that sounds like me" while reading this book, speak with your doctor to get the support you need.

Self-care starts with the belief that you are valuable. Let this book uplift, validate, and encourage you because you *are* valuable! So, get ready to experience the healing powers of self-care!

CHAPTER ONE
Emotional Self-Care

People with ADHD need to be especially mindful of their emotional needs as they navigate through the journey of managing their symptoms. Due to emotional dysregulation, you struggle with feelings that seem bigger, more intense, and harder to control. You may be more easily impacted by other people's emotional climates. You may also struggle with feelings of shame and guilt, as you have limited control over your responses to emotionally demanding situations. This is why self-care—the actions you take to connect with your emotions and process them in a healthy way—is so vital.

In this chapter, you will learn how to nurture your own emotional needs. The activities described here will allow you to learn more about the intricacies and subtle nuances of the ADHD brain and how to utilize them to tend to your emotional landscape. These simple and actionable practices are meant to be repeated as often as needed and incorporated into a routine as you progress forward. A few emotional self-care activities you will find in this chapter are reframing your idea of failure, challenging negative thoughts, celebrating small wins, and focusing on gratitude. Responding to your emotional needs may not come naturally at first, but it becomes easier and more fulfilling as you learn to integrate it into your life. By regularly engaging in emotional self-care and employing self-compassion, you can develop healthy coping mechanisms that greatly enhance your joy and sense of well-being.

Find What You Are Grateful For

Gratitude is the thankful appreciation for what you have and receive. It is a way of acknowledging the good in your life. Focusing on gratitude is a foolproof way to become more connected with positive emotions, to handle adversity, and to cultivate healthy relationships. Here are tips about practicing gratitude:

- **It's not just for big things.** Be mindful of and appreciative for any good thing—big or small—that happens. Gratitude teaches you to reframe the way you view things: exploring and appreciating the good instead of ignoring it and focusing on the bad.

- **Practice mindfulness.** Learning to slow down your overactive, busy brain and really luxuriate in thinking about five to ten good things currently happening may help you become happier and experience deeper empathy. You can train your brain to be more conscious of things to be grateful about with repeated practice.

- **Help others.** An awareness of where other people need aid coupled with the ability to help them can immediately boost your well-being, which intrinsically makes you more capable of feeling gratitude. It also serves as a good reminder to cherish what you often take for granted.

Gratitude seems like it should be second nature to us, but it is actually a carefully curated skill. The key is to set some time aside and practice (I do it right before bed as a way of recapping my day). Try to think about some things you are grateful for and start your gratitude practice today.

Challenge Negative Thoughts

Most people have an ongoing dialogue with themselves. Positive self-talk can improve your mood and confidence and enhance your productivity. Negative self-talk can do the opposite, and, when coupled with self-doubt inherently caused by ADHD, it can be challenging to reframe things in a realistic way.

Evolutionarily speaking, negative self-talk is a part of the human experience. We are hardwired with a negativity bias, which means our brains tell us we are more likely to experience negative versus positive stimuli. This is our mind's way of protecting us from inherent threats. However, if left unchecked, negativity can be consuming.

Challenging negative thoughts is a disciplined practice of reframing your negative self-talk to create a positive shift in your mentality. Here are a few tips to challenge your indefatigable inner critic.

1. **Become aware of negative self-talk.** Understand what the thought is, when you are having it, and why it is happening. This can be the first step in halting this automatic spiral into the negative.

2. **Dispute the thought.** Think of hard evidence that disproves the thought you are having.

3. **Prioritize effort over outcome.** By shifting the emphasis on how hard you try to do something, you may be able to detach yourself from catastrophizing about competency or ability.

4. **Be kind to yourself.** Accepting that you are imperfect and still worthy of self-compassion is something we all could benefit from.

Allow Yourself to De-Mask

ADHD masking is when someone with ADHD presents in a way that makes them seem like they are not living with the disorder. This occurs in roughly a third of people with ADHD and disproportionately in women. Masking involves conscious and unconscious methods of camouflaging symptoms by mimicking behaviors of neurotypical people. People mask because it helps them to blend into society more seamlessly and bypass the stigma and judgment of their diagnosis.

ADHD masking is a way of hiding symptoms through learned behaviors. This can be normal and adaptive or unhealthy and limiting. Many people with ADHD have been forced to mask parts of themselves that society deems as unacceptable. This may be tenable for short periods, but, eventually, the weight of the mask becomes too heavy to bear.

Masking can lead to negative impacts like a delay in diagnosis, or people not validating your experience when you tell them you are struggling. In working so hard to mask, you may develop alternative coping skills that might lead you down the road to anxiety, depression, or substance abuse. Perhaps the most tragic consequence of masking is a loss of self. It may be hard to distinguish between what is you and what is the act you are putting on for other people.

But what can you do when masking becomes who you are? If you can identify when masking is taking place, you can start implementing new skills to cope, without having to create a more "acceptable" persona.

One of the first things to do is understand which of your masking behaviors are healthy (like finding an alternative way of fidgeting to be less obvious or mimicking other people's facial expressions in a conversation) and which are detrimental (for example, allowing other people to talk in conversation versus never speaking for fear your opinion may differ from what it is "supposed" to be).

Secondly, process through your emotions instead of avoiding them. A skilled therapist can help you navigate these emotionally laden waters. Sometimes, just allowing yourself to feel what you are feeling rather than rushing to cover it up is a vital step.

Find and enjoy a safe place. If you have found that you are masking, build time into your day where you can be your genuine self. Eventually, the disparity between the real you and your mask will grow, and you will gain the comfort to start unmasking in other situations. You may find that when this happens, it feels as though a weight has been lifted, as there is a certain freedom in living authentically.

Notice Your Inner Experience

People with ADHD often have difficulty interpreting their own internal environment. They can inadequately process emotional data, especially when it is coupled with robust physiological responses (rapid heart rate, facial flushing, muscle tension). For neurotypical people, this is a concerted performance that delivers data to your brain to guide behavior. In neurodivergent brains, this may be a staggered, erratic process that leaves you trying to interpret physical symptoms without understanding the underlying emotional trigger.

Alternatively (and perhaps more infuriatingly), people with ADHD deal with difficulty naming the emotion because all we feel is a sense of urgency. That makes it hard to figure out the appropriate course of action, as we may not know if we are fulfilled or bored, frustrated or disappointed, angry or embarrassed. Emotion involves interpreting physiological signals (elevated heart rate, for example). However, we are susceptible to inherent biases that cause us to misread ambiguous signals as dangerous ones.

Misinterpreted emotional information is a difficult and draining part of the ADHD experience. Through heightened awareness and coping skills (and professional help, if available), it is possible to better understand your mental milieu. Working on this skill set leads to greater emotional resilience and better communication, and it can significantly improve the quality of your life. Learning how your brain works helps you steer your life toward optimal success.

Throughout this process, just remain mindful that you always were and always will be so much more than the areas where you struggle.

Don't Dwell On Lost Time

One of the hardest things about being diagnosed later in life is the feeling that you have *lost* time. ADHD is commonly "skipped" or misdiagnosed because it is hard to diagnose intelligent adults who have developed coping skills to mask their deficits.

It can be hard to conceptualize the idea of missing a diagnosis when internally the struggle seems so apparent. However, maybe it's not just a diagnostic error. Maybe some of the delay is because you were told your entire life that you weren't living up to expectations, and now there is some trepidation about seeking treatment that validates that your brain is "broken."

Maybe the deficit becomes so damaging that you finally take the first step. You work hard to advocate for yourself after years of failing to be heard. You get diagnosed, you get treated, and things finally feel like they should.

And *now* the grief sets in. Why didn't I do this sooner? I wasted so much time before treatment! Imagine what life could have been like.

Don't let yesterday's grief make you miss today's opportunity. Mourning the loss of time can be appropriate, but it often gets in the way of celebrating the opportunity of facing the world in a new way. It is entirely possible that in the time before adequately managing your ADHD, you were building coping skills that now you can utilize fully. It was not *lost* time; it was just a different time.

Write in a Journal

Journaling was something that I really enjoyed doing but had a lot of difficulty maintaining. I would get frustrated with myself for picking it up and giving it up so many times, especially when I felt like it was almost immediately beneficial every time.

So why is writing things in a journal such a helpful practice for those with ADHD?

1. **It helps you slow down.** Journaling allows you to decelerate enough to clear out and organize your brain. The ADHD brain works circularly when it is overstimulated. It just spins around wildly and very rarely lands on a solution. When you can write down your thoughts, fears, and concerns, you can process them in a more leisurely fashion. After rereading my entries, I almost always came to a conclusion about what I wrote down (I also write things down when I am upset with someone so I can organize my thoughts, so be concerned if you get a written letter from me).

2. **It helps you recognize patterns.** The other benefit is that journaling allows you to recognize your patterns, especially in the context of sequential entries. This is almost like witnessing your life from an external perspective because you have the benefit of looking at what you wrote as important, whereas you may forget those details as time progresses, which makes it hard to identify a pattern.

3. **It helps you process through emotions more effectively.** Due to the emotional dysregulation that happens with ADHD, it is common to have certain cognitive distortion about your

experiences. Journaling is helpful because you can almost become an impartial party to what is going on, writing facts and then processing accordingly.

Just be mindful when you start your journaling to treat yourself with compassion. No one wants to reread a laundry list of their failures. This is a tool to encourage, inspire, and help you cope healthily with your steady flow of active thoughts. It's okay to write about things that weren't great, but this is not a medium for you to further drag yourself down with negative self-talk. Who is that helping?

By the way, if you look at a blank journal and freeze because it is almost too much commitment to put words into such a pristine, blank vessel, then find another way that works. It doesn't have to be pen and paper. Hammer away on your laptop. Do digital voice recordings. Record a personal vlog or create a social media channel (not a public channel; do this just for you!). There are tons of ways to get benefit from this exercise. Don't get tied up by the word "journaling"...it doesn't actually have to be in a journal.

Listen to Music

I can tell you right now, I have never successfully mastered an instrument (in fourth grade, I got a reed of a clarinet stuck in my lip and have never ventured back), but I love music. Listening to music has been restorative, healing, and stabilizing for me. But why is music so helpful for ADHD brains?

The rhythm and tempo of music are thought to modulate some symptoms of inattentiveness. Learning to play an instrument can also help develop skills needed for attention regulation, impulse control, and forward decision-making. It may also enhance your ability to work in a noisy environment, which is useful for coping with distractions.

For some people, listening to music during task-oriented activities works well because it keeps you activated, focused, and less prone to distractions. Play around and explore different genres, as different types of music can evoke different emotional responses. An upbeat, catchy song can stimulate the brain and increase dopamine levels. A slowed-down ballad or instrumental interlude can calm and soothe you, bringing you out of an elevated state.

Another way music can be a wonderful tool in your self-care arsenal is to manage time blindness. Often it is easier and more enjoyable to build time perception by gauging progression through a song instead of a standard, under-stimulating clock. Cleaning, chores, and other relatively mindless tasks can be made more engaging and stimulating if you are participating alongside a soundtrack.

Reframe Your Views about Failure

There is nothing in life that I fear more than failure. From a young age, I was repeatedly told that I needed to avoid failure at all costs, yet I constantly felt the weight of ADHD slowly pushing me underwater. I felt every failure to be evidence of my incompetence and proof of my inabilities, and each one got inscribed into my nervous system for me to relive at any given moment.

But perhaps I was wrong. Maybe I just need to reframe this concept in my brain. But how? How do I take this belief, which seems so intrinsic to my being, and just "think" of it another way?

1. **Let that fear motivate you.** The fear of failure can keep you pushing forward. It can keep that active, engaged, creative mind thinking out of the box and achieving in the most unlikely of circumstances.

2. **Don't let it paralyze you.** Your brain naturally rejects ambivalence. It does not want to constantly be stuck in "what if" patterns driven by fear. Fear of failure is natural, but don't let it prevent you from taking those initial steps.

3. **Learn from your failures.** What did you do wrong? More importantly, what did you do *right*? The second time around, you will be better prepared to handle it differently.

Express Yourself Through Poetry

Poetry holds a very therapeutic role because you can process through a dense emotional cloud and use that to *create* something that expresses that turmoil through words. It can foster emotional expression so you can better understand your feelings. Through this expression, you are utilizing parts of your brain that help massage that emotion into something more supple and malleable.

Poetry has been an almost spiritual release for me. It has pulled me through some deep despair (and deeper healing), broken relationships, and confusing achievements. It even helped me process and understand my ADHD at a time when I was too scared to examine my internal environment. Rather than continue to tell you the benefits, I will just share this poem with you:

Love Story to the ADHD Brain

This is a love story to the chaos of the mind,
An ode to those that struggle and grind,
An explanation to voyagers who have grown weary,
Of trudging through fog, so dense and so dreary.

For those who feel mired in a tangled mess,
Forced to choose between order and happiness,
Foolishly labeled as lazy or thoughtless,
Held to standards of homes that are spotless.

Thoughts slip away like water through fingers,
Guilt and shame ensue and self-doubt lingers
Reinventing the process with hopes for a change,
Falling short yet again, target is never in range.

For those who feel destined to aimlessly drift,
Through tumultuous currents that widen the rift
Between who they are and who they could be
A contrast so glaring for all to now see.

Unraveling at the thought of a tedious task,
Petrified with fear of lowering their mask,
And allowing people to witness the state of their being,
Anticipating the rejection when people start seeing.

Putting on a cloak to hide what's inside,
Dreams of authenticity roll away with the tide,
A brilliant impostor, an elaborate swindle,
Pushed to pretend, the real self starts to dwindle.

And sometimes in these darkest times,
We lean on stories, dreams, and rhymes,
To give us hope, to feel understood and heard,
To validate emotion through written word.

For the people who have continued to push upstream,
And sacrificed for their chance at the dream,
The mind is not static: It changes and evolves.
Fueled by goodness, around which it revolves.

Continue to fearlessly move to whatever seems out of reach,
Be brave in your movements, your thoughts, your speech,
Breathe in the confidence with all you've been through
The mind is unique.

No one can do what you do.

Leave Behind the "Superpower" Rhetoric

"ADHD is my superpower" is truly something I never want to hear again. I understand the motivation behind reframing things into a positive light. And if that is what you truly believe, I applaud you. Honestly, I am even low-key jealous that you feel that way about your brain.

If given the choice of whether I want ADHD or not, ten out of ten times I would pick the latter. I do appreciate some positives of ADHD, but I dream of the simplicity of a life where my brain wasn't moving ten thousand miles per hour all the time.

When people attempt to reframe this as a superpower, I find it to be toxic positivity. I feel like it minimizes the struggles of people who simply can't reframe things due to the severity of their symptoms. I feel like it indicates that struggles will simply go away if you voluntarily think about them in a more positive way. I think we need to just be realistic about it.

Some days my brain is utterly amazing, but some days it is total garbage. Instead of telling myself that every day should be remarkable because I have this "superpower," I look at the situation with an emotion-neutral observation: "This is how my brain is wired. It is neither good nor bad; it just is what it is. I don't need it to function perfectly all the time, and I am grateful that I am able to do what I am doing today."

Navigate Through Anxiety

So often people are scared to address ADHD because of underlying anxiety. And I get it; that's scary. But sometimes people have anxiety *due to their* ADHD. I know for me, it presents as near panic when I get overwhelmed by things to do or overstimulated by chaotic places, or when I'm running behind. This is part of why it is important to get an appropriate and comprehensive diagnosis (if it's accessible), because ADHD can be so nuanced and subtle and can look like a lot of different things.

The comorbidity (more than one medical condition existing simultaneously) of anxiety and ADHD is well documented, but it is hard to figure out if these are truly two separate conditions or if one is masking the other. One of the first questions in assessing anxiety and ADHD is: Is your anxiety caused by your inability to focus, or is your inability to focus caused by your anxiety? That provides more clarity on where the anxiety is coming from, but the sad truth is that a lot of people with ADHD have to deal with anxiety. There are times when my ADHD catapults me into an absolute frenzy. When that happens, it becomes nearly impossible to organize my thoughts enough to sort out what I truly need to be anxious about, so I get anxious about *everything*. Self-care activities like drinking enough water, reducing caffeine, and addressing medication (if appropriate) can help.

Celebrate Your Small Wins

Let's talk about goals. Goals are what we use to propel us forward and give our lives greater meaning. For ADHD people, goals can seem unattainable because we simply run out of steam trying to reach them. Why does that happen? Why, even when it is something we desperately want, are we telling ourselves that this is too big of a challenge to undertake?

We are built to see the negative. We want to fixate on the problems and the errors and use them as a gauge of our progress. Often, one bad thing can drown out ten positive things of equal measure. The most problematic thing about this mindset is that it can feed you a narrative that results in giving up your dreams.

Highly successful people don't necessarily fail less. They just have a healthier mindset regarding failure and their goals. Did you know that it took Thomas Edison ten thousand attempts to create the light bulb? When asked about his "failures" before his eventual success, he said, "I have not failed. I've just found ten thousand ways that won't work." Through reframing those negatives, he was able to gather data and create success because his mindset was filtered through what he could achieve, not how he had failed.

A pivotal part of that intrinsic shift in mentality is celebrating your small wins. There are numerous incremental steps that lead you to your big wins. The ADHD brain runs on immediate gratification. So when you attempt to conceptualize goals that are far away, it is hard to gauge what you need to get you to the finish line. Often, the thought of potentially not experiencing the grand reward in the immediate future is enough to shut off the motivation tap.

Celebrating those small milestones lights up the brain and fires off that dopamine that signals to the rest of the brain that you should keep going! It is through that persistent stepwise pattern that you can get to your next big achievement.

At any given point, your journey through ADHD may be invalidated by people who deny that ADHD is legitimate, or feel like it is overdiagnosed, or feel like medications give an unfair advantage. My wish for them is that they one day realize what a massive accomplishment it is to manage such an impressively busy brain. My wish for you is that you learn to celebrate your small wins. See how far you have come. Soak and revel in achieving what other people had deemed impossible for you.

Make a Vision Board

You don't have to get out magazines and posterboard and glitter, but you may benefit from a creative expression of displaying your goals visually. The underlying thought behind these images is to have your goals in front of you so you can be mindful of what you are striving for.

This may seem like a childish practice to you. You may be feigning interest and going through the motions as you cut and paste. But this is not about the end product. This is meant to be a process in mindfulness where you are assessing what is truly important to you.

The ADHD brain is beautifully circuitous. People whose brains function more linearly and in a grid-based manner may not understand the labyrinthine mental associations that take us from thought A to thought B. This is part of why a vision board can be so fun. It sparks diverse neural connections, and it is a creative way to organize your goals and dreams.

This is a little different from "manifesting what you want." Just because you put pictures together doesn't mean that the universe is going to align to give you those things. You can have thoughts and dreams, but it is up to you to put them into action. As the Cheshire Cat said, "If you don't know where you're going, any road will get you there." Don't let that creepy cat be right. Visualize and actionize your plans.

Learn to Forgive Yourself

Forgiveness is not something that comes easily to me. I have a fragile ego bolstered by excessive pride, and then on top of that, I handle rejection extremely poorly. However, as reluctant as I am to provide forgiveness to everyone else, I am even less likely to bestow it upon myself.

I think it stems from the fact that I just wanted my brain to be "normal." I struggled with the knowledge of knowing *what* my brain is supposed to do and the inevitable disappointment when it does not cooperate. I have reconciled and learned to accept and appropriately manage my symptoms, but it has taken me a long time not to spin down a shame cycle when faced with failure. I remind myself that my frontal lobe (in charge of decision-making and course-correcting and learning from errors) is wired differently. I repeat to myself that my ADHD is not who I am but just one aspect of my brain's functioning. I adhere to self-care routines, organizational structures, and a strict diet and exercise schedule, but sometimes things still don't work.

And that is why self-compassion is perhaps the most vital thing you should take from this book. It is the best tool against that subversive current of shame that threatens your very foundation. Recognizing your truth: that you are doing your best and deserve to be taken care of and nurtured. Learning to forgive yourself will most likely be the thing that helps you accomplish your goals despite those setbacks.

Reflect On Childhood ADHD

It is estimated that only 10 percent of adults grow out of their childhood ADHD. If you received your diagnosis as an adult or suspect as an adult that you have ADHD, you can likely look back on your childhood and pinpoint certain elements or memories where you felt different from your peers; where it was harder for you to complete certain tasks, focus in ways others could, or regulate your energy levels. And maybe your ADHD got you into trouble for not focusing or creating distractions for yourself at inappropriate moments, which further distanced you from your peers.

I was diagnosed with ADHD in fourth grade after I formed a coup in my classroom. I got the other kids to stand on their desks and chant at our poor, unsuspecting educator. That is one example of (unfortunately) many times when my younger self was "troublesome," "disruptive," or (the one that stuck with me forever) "consistently inconsistent." Perhaps you were labeled this way during your childhood as well. What those various grievances didn't encapsulate was the fact that you were struggling with an attention disorder, and that you were a smart, creative, rambunctious child who got bored easily and sought ways to entertain themself, just as I was.

As a child, you probably didn't understand why you were different, why things had to be harder for you when it seemed that everyone else could get by easily. You may not have understood the difference between yourself and neurotypical children and blamed yourself for these "short-comings." And others, including adults, most likely treated you with a lack of compassion because of their own lack of understanding.

Looking back on this feeling of ostracization can be difficult and/or triggering for you as an adult, but I encourage you to look back on experiences where you were not given compassion with your ADHD or where you didn't hold compassion for yourself, and where you or others were holding you to an unfair neurotypical standard. Imagine speaking to your younger self during these difficult moments and telling yourself it is okay to not be neurotypical, and, more importantly, it is okay to be a child with ADHD. These moments are what led to where you are today.

Knowing what you know now about your ADHD, what would you say to comfort yourself then? What would you say to comfort yourself now?

Recognize Your Triggers

People with ADHD have a very active and engaged nervous system. This means that seemingly benign comments or inputs incite a massive biological response that may be difficult to control. This is part of the reason it is so important to recognize your triggers, so you can learn how to avoid or better manage situations in which emotional regulation may be an issue.

First, it is important to understand the concept of a trigger. An emotional trigger is anything that sparks an intense emotional reaction, regardless of your current mood. Sometimes, due to impairments in working memory, a fleeting emotion can flood the brain with one powerful emotion, rendering you incapable of logically processing your way through.

Currently, emotional dysregulation is not even included in the diagnostic criteria for ADHD. Many doctors are not trained to look for those nuances, which is part of the reason ADHD frequently gets misdiagnosed as a mood disorder. Often, people are left to fend for themselves as they burn with frustration, anger, and emotional lability.

Being able to assess what triggers you is important because it differs from person to person. Start to investigate what causes you to emotionally "flood," and keep a log on your phone or in a journal. Eventually, you may start to notice patterns with timing, environment, or specific people. Track back to see the triggers: impulsive behavior, frustration/impatience, feelings of rejection or disapproval, and anxiety. By understanding your own emotional triggers, you will be better equipped to preempt those situations.

Reflect On Positive Qualities and Strengths

Neurodivergent brains are expected to perform in a neurotypical world, but trying to force a square peg into a round hole can be endlessly frustrating. It also dilutes some of the incredible positives that come with having ADHD.

Some of these strengths that deserve to be celebrated are:

- Creativity. Being blessed with this ability to see things from a different perspective can make you better at problem-solving and innovation. People with ADHD are usually imaginative, artistic, and original.

- High energy. This seemingly endless source of energy can be a huge plus when it comes to having stamina for long projects (especially ones you are interested in!).

- Resilience. Despite the constant barrage of "areas of improvement" and repeated disappointments, people with ADHD manage to persist. We can push past roadblocks, change and adapt on a dime, and learn from the experiences that lead us to eventual successes.

- Possessing hyperfocus. People with ADHD have these bright flashes of brilliance that allow us to focus so intently on a task that the rest of the world melts away. The advantage of this is being able to channel your attention and energy into your work when many others have had to stop (I am currently writing this—and many other chapters—in a burst of hyperfocus).

Is there something truly exceptional that you attribute to your ADHD?

Be Proactive about Depressive Episodes

The catastrophic thing about ADHD is that it cleverly mimics other mood disorders. Then, to further convolute matters, depression can worsen focus, and ADHD can impact depression, so it is even more complicated to understand the pathology of this condition.

When you are attempting to push through the cognitive mud of depression, it is hard to believe you are ever going to get out of it. You feel emotionally and mentally mired in this low place, and it is hard to understand the steps required to extract yourself. The last thing you feel capable of is making major life changes. That is why it is so important to try to preempt these episodes.

The first step is recognizing how you *feel* when depression starts to creep in. Depression can manifest physically. It can decrease your energy, leaving you feeling drained. It can cause brain fog, which makes it harder to process or commit things to memory. It can change your sleep cycle, so you are either sleeping all the time or barely at all. It can alter your appetite, and you can vacillate between forgetting to eat or emotionally bingeing. Noticing symptoms and body cues early help you prevent this transient moment of depression from turning into a full-blown episode.

Recognizing symptoms may be one thing, but recognizing what to do is a completely different challenge. Having to navigate those turbulent tides alone can be difficult. It can be hard to think clearly and craft and execute a plan to overcome these feelings. In a particularly cruel twist of fate, it is also increasingly difficult to reach out for help because you feel guilty and ashamed for feeling that way or because you are just too tired to expend the emotional energy to explain what is going on. This causes withdrawal and isolation and makes things exponentially worse.

Reaching out and vocalizing this silent burden is not a sign of weakness. This can actually put you in a spot of greater autonomy in terms of managing your symptoms because you are actively staying connected to others and taking part in social activities.

It also helps to keep in mind what you used to enjoy. There is a phenomenon of depression called *anhedonia*, which is the inability to feel pleasure in pleasurable activities. When you are amid that, it might be hard to think about what would relax and energize you because nothing is lighting up that neural circuitry. Rely instead on doing things you used to enjoy. Even if the depression doesn't lift immediately, it is one of the best shots you have at triggering that joy cascade.

And for the sake of completeness, if you are working on behavioral modification and self-care but still find your depression getting worse, you should seek professional care. Depression is a neuropsychiatric condition that is *treatable*, so if you have concerns, go see your doctor.

Engage In a Social Justice Issue

Sometimes the best way to grow from inward is to focus outward. Given this era of politicized movements and misinformation campaigns, a lot of noise gets made about the wrong things. People can gain a tremendous amount of benefit from knowing they have advocated for a cause they feel passionate about. This is an *extremely* useful way to funnel those extraneous ADHD skills.

When focusing on a purpose bigger than yourself, a couple of things happen. You stimulate your brain and trigger a rush of dopamine, which continues to propel you forward. This can lend itself to increased zeal and fervor and help push you toward making some real progress for change. We also find a way to reconcile the internal issues within ourselves so we can make space to deal with the external situations happening around us.

The most important things to keep in mind before jumping into advocacy is to educate yourself on the topic and to know your boundaries. One of the most frustrating things about highly contentious social issues is the absolute deluge of information to sift through. Getting information from trusted sources will help fuel your passion responsibly.

But when that surge of stimulation happens because you pursue something you are passionate about, it can sometimes be hard to know when to stop. It is important to recognize your own boundaries and when you are reaching your emotional threshold so that you can avoid getting overwhelmed.

Don't Live in Denial

What you have been experiencing has a name: attention deficit hyperactivity disorder. Reconcile with this diagnosis because once you identify it, understand it, and explore it, then you can *manage* it. Living in denial only hurts you.

Many adults who have ADHD don't know they have it. They have been simply surviving, thinking that what they are experiencing is normal or not problematic enough to address. They may have been silently struggling with school, work, and relationships for a majority of their lives.

What about those who started to suspect ADHD? Maybe they saw something on social media that resonated with them, or saw similar symptoms in their child, or just grew tired of the relentless grind to maintain basic functionality? But what happens when they bring it up to friends and family or even their doctor, and their concerns are not validated? Does the journey stop there?

No. You are your own best advocate and the best judge of your internal environment. When people talk about how ADHD isn't that big of a deal (or other invalidating platitudes), I feel it viscerally. I think about how much it took from me and how much it takes to continue to manage it. But it can be done, and accepting that you may have it is the first step. It is never too late to seek a diagnosis and treatment for ADHD. Effective treatment can make life easier, not only for you but for your family as well.

Control Your Anger

Anger is an extremely volatile and unstable emotion to attempt to manage, especially if you already struggle with emotional regulation. Have you felt like you feel things with a greater intensity than people around you? Or that you are too sensitive? Or that you are overreacting?

People with ADHD are more prone to intense emotional fluctuations. This may be due to poor impulse control (showing poor judgment in how they express their anger or heightened difficultly de-escalating when they do get angry); intensified frustration due to issues with executive function (executive function refers to the mental processes that enable us to plan, initiate, and sustain focus and juggle multiple goal-directed tasks successfully); feeling overwhelmed; attention difficulties (getting easily distracted by something that makes you angry); or difficulty navigating through conflict due to impaired social cues.

Often, we don't recognize that we are becoming irate until we feel the uncomfortable physical feelings of that rush of anger: the facial flushing, the sense that your whole body is overheating, the sudden muscle tension and trembling.

So how do we recognize and manage anger in a timely and effective way?

- **Understand your triggers.** To adequately manage the emotion, you need to know the situations that make you angry. Anger is a natural and valid human emotion, and it is normal to feel angry in response to unfairness, maltreatment, and frustration. Identifying your anger triggers in unavoidable situations, preparing yourself ahead of time, and utilizing deep breathing and muscle relaxation in the moment can help.

- **Remove yourself from the situation.** If you feel yourself escalating, walk away. Leave before you react impulsively or say or do something irrevocable. For many people with ADHD, the impulsive behavior that anger causes can be even more destructive and start that downward spiral. Even if a person cannot control their emotions, they can control their reactions. A good rule is to commit to delay reacting until you feel calm.

- **Separate yourself from the emotion.** Your anger is an emotional signal telling your brain that something is not right. Learning to look at objective facts instead of fixating on the rising fury helps you articulate more appropriately and resolve the issue faster and more effectively.

- **Set good boundaries.** People with ADHD generally have issues with setting and maintaining personal boundaries. Crossing these boundaries can be the thing that sets off this anger cascade, yet your friend or partner might be totally oblivious to the transgression if you never asserted that this was a firm boundary. Learning how to enforce boundaries rather than emotionally responding when they have been violated is pivotal.

Recognize Emotional Dysregulation

People with ADHD tend to experience emotions robustly but have difficulties regulating and responding appropriately. Awareness of this dysfunction in self-regulation can bypass a lot of impairment.

Here are some key areas where emotional dysregulation may be present:

- **Emotional impulsivity.** Due to an inability to inhibit inappropriate thoughts, statements, and behaviors, you are left to deal with impatience, anger and frustration, inappropriate emotional responses, and heightened excitability.

- **Inability to self-soothe.** There is a breakdown in de-escalation after a vigorous emotion that leaves you suspended in this high-alert mode until you exhaust your mental resources or until you are distracted by something else.

- **Inability to refocus attention.** It is easy to ruminate or rehash details about things that are emotionally provocative, which makes it harder to process logically or conceptualize the next steps.

- **Difficulty implementing healthy responses.** Sometimes it is simply not feasible to coordinate an action plan when you are in that heightened emotional state. You might risk replacing healthier choices that are more aligned with future plans with things that temporarily satisfy short-term goals.

It is important to be cognizant of this neural phenomenon, as it provides us with a base of self-compassion if/when your emotions get the best of you.

CHAPTER TWO
Physical Self-Care

Physical self-care is most likely what you think about when you hear the blanket term "self-care." We all know the fundamental tenets of eating healthily, exercising regularly, and sleeping soundly, but what you may not know is how that impacts the ADHD brain in particular. You may not fully conceptualize the importance of taking care of your overall health as a means of managing your symptoms.

Taking care of your body may not be at the top of your priority lists for many reasons. You may feel like you don't have time to make changes or that you might be overwhelmed by how far you must go to become "healthy." You may lean on your predisposition for instant gratification and give up building habits because you aren't seeing immediate improvement. You may even feel like taking care of yourself is too self-indulgent and you haven't earned that luxury.

Taking care of yourself isn't a luxury. It's a means of survival. In this chapter, you will find activities that will help you find your own form of physical self-care. Some of those include finding an exercise you like and can maintain, staying hydrated, incorporating good sleep hygiene, and learning how to modulate your caffeine intake. Being mindful and making small, gradual changes to your physical health can help you optimize your global functioning.

Hydrate

Water is vital to almost every biological process in the body. It is pivotal in delivering nutrients to the brain so that it has the energy to keep going. When you start to get dehydrated, your blood volume drops, which causes your blood pressure to drop. Your body attempts to compensate for the lack of water by raising your heart rate and altering your kidney function to retain more water. That's a lot of work to maintain simple body functioning.

Ensuring that you are adequately hydrated prevents the inevitable brain fog, mood swings, and executive dysfunction that comes with water depletion.

For those of you that forget to drink water, feel overwhelmed with the amount of water you need to drink, or think water "tastes boring," these tips are for you:

- Have a big water bottle within arm's reach and visual distance to you. If it is ready and waiting in front of you, you are more likely to reach for it and drink it.

- Drink one glass of water as soon as you wake up. This is also beneficial for digestion, because we all know dehydration can lead to constipation (which is a hell I choose to avoid).

- Make your water interesting. Add fruit. Put in flavored ice (mint is great!). Make lemonade. Just get that water in.

Practice Yoga

When I was in medical school (at the height of navigating through ADHD and everything else in life), I had a hard time staying "tethered." In that state of chaos and crisis, I felt like I had nothing to hold on to to stabilize me. I tried to use other people to anchor me, but that only gave me temporary relief. Then I started doing yoga.

From a neurobiological process standpoint, people who regularly practice yoga have functional improvements in the brain areas responsible for memory (hippocampus), emotional regulation (amygdala), and executive function (prefrontal cortex).

Yoga is all about slowing down. Flowing through movements and poses encourages breathing deeply, stretching the body, and focusing intently. Its core tenets are based on mindfulness, which is perhaps the most enriching part of this form of ADHD management. It requires you to pull your focus inward to concentrate on your breathing and to pay attention to your body. By listening to those cues, you become more present and grounded within the moment and are more capable of harnessing your attention.

By dedicating time to practice mindfulness, you can learn how to regulate those highly combustible thoughts and respond to them in a calm and balanced way. It is an excellent way to manage stress and truly focus on well-being in a comprehensive sense.

Find an Exercise You Like

I hate working out. I hate sweating. I have never gotten a "runner's high." Most times I have joined a gym, I will go for the social component for the first few weeks, and then I'm a ghost. However, I know I need exercise so I can function more completely (check out the "Practice Yoga" entry in this chapter!).

Exercise is beneficial for a plethora of reasons, but for people with ADHD, working out can simultaneously reduce hyperactivity, enhance attention and memory, and promote relaxation. It is perhaps the most positive way to modify your neural wiring to achieve a more consistent state of stability.

Areas of the brain that regulate the stress response, including the amygdala and prefrontal cortex, are calmed during exercise. When you are emotionally overloaded, exercise can reduce that neural chaos so you can process more effectively. When you engage in strenuous physical activity, you're fundamentally imitating the physical responses that can come with anxiety, allowing you to adapt and learn how to manage these responses and not be overwhelmed by them when they come up organically.

Exercising leads to higher circulating levels of dopamine and more available dopamine receptors. This remodeling of the reward system also plays a key role in regulating the attention system. In addition to promoting alertness, it helps shift and redirect attention more appropriately, thus protecting you from distraction.

So here are some tips to get some exercise in:

- Try to find something you like. The more engaging the exercise is, the more likely you will be to continue it. So maybe exercise with a friend; work out to music you enjoy; or take a class, if that might make you feel more accountable.

- Try to exercise regularly (preferably daily). You don't have to do anything formal, just something to get your body moving. You may consider doing some free directed exercises on *YouTube* or follow fitness instructors on social media.

- Try to be outside. If this is an accessible option, it's nice to spend some time outside in the sun and fresh air. It indicates to your body that you are doing something for yourself and enhances some of the positive regulatory benefits of exercise.

Again, you're probably not going to suddenly get into bodybuilding form; just focus on making small, progressive changes. Remember the message here is learning to take small, actionable steps toward better self-care and symptom management. And if all that fails, work out because it will give you an excuse to get some cute athleisure wear.

Change Your Relationship with Medication

Let's talk about the "right" medication. The right medication is what is right *for you*. There are so many factors to consider, including your genetics, your underlying psychiatric conditions, your current life situations, and your financial situation. This is not a one-size-fits-all situation.

In a way, that's oddly comforting to me. I like the theory that anyone can personalize and find a perfect fit for their medication. However, the journey can be very laborious. In medical school, it took me seven different medications before I found "the one." (And to complicate things, "the one" can be different at different points of your life, but that's for another time....)

First, let me say that medication is one of many treatment options and is not an appropriate choice for everyone. If this is a treatment modality that you and your physician decide is right for you, having a healthy and mindful relationship with medication is important. Medication is not going to "solve" your ADHD. Medication can be a potent tool in your arsenal, but you get maximum efficacy when you pair that with appropriate behavioral modification and self-care.

I can earnestly say that if I hadn't incorporated nonmedication options and behavioral management with my medication, I probably wouldn't have been able to complete school. It's vital to build those good pathways and habits so you don't have to rely as heavily on medication.

If you have tried medication, did it take numerous attempts to find the right fit? Are you still looking?

Take Your Vitamins

On a basic level, vitamins can be extremely beneficial. Recognizing the nutritional benefits of certain vitamins is helpful in supplementing your diet, but occasionally (especially with ADHD), deficiencies persist. Being aware of these vitamins and their specific benefits for ADHD brains may be a worthwhile conversation to have with your physician:

- Zinc. This helps regulate dopamine in the brain, and data show that it can reduce hyperactivity and impulsivity. Zinc is found in beef, shrimp, pumpkin seeds, and spinach.

- Magnesium. This supplement helps with sleep, relaxation, anxiety, and digestion. It aids the neurotransmitters to better address attentional issues. You can find magnesium in nuts, seeds, beans, and dark, leafy greens.

- Vitamin B. This vitamin promotes alertness while decreasing anxiety. Signs of deficiency include fatigue and irritability. Look for vitamin B in bananas, spinach, and salmon.

- Iron. Data shows that low iron levels can exacerbate ADHD symptoms. It is important to note that taking too much iron can be detrimental (and constipating). If you want to boost iron naturally, great iron-rich foods are dark chocolate, leafy greens, and red meat.

- Vitamin C. Vitamin C can help synthesize neurotransmitters, but you should proceed with caution if you are on certain ADHD medications, as too much vitamin C can interfere with the absorption of those medications.

Take a Walk

Long walks on the beach aren't just dating profile clichés; they are objectively therapeutic for you. They are low impact and require no specialized skill, equipment, or facility. As we have touched on throughout this book, the ADHD brain is highly impacted by your overall health. When everything is optimized and working together, you have better control of your symptoms and lead a happier, healthier, less chaotic life.

There are numerous benefits of walking. It can improve your mood in as little as thirty minutes of walking per day. It improves sleep quality and potently reduces stress, anxiety, and fatigue. Physically active people are at a significantly reduced risk of becoming depressed, and exercise during a depressive episode can help you reduce the severity and length of symptoms.

The physical improvements you achieve by walking are notable as well. Walking supports weight loss and improves cardiovascular health. It can also enhance your perception of body image and confidence. Staying active can improve cognitive function, memory, attention, and processing speed. Older people who stay active can reduce their risk of cognitive decline and dementia.

When you look at the benefits of walking specifically for ADHD, you see that it boosts mood and general functioning by increasing blood flow and circulation to the brain and body. It feeds oxygen and nutrients more efficiently into the central nervous system and soothes your hyperactive stress response.

There is an additional benefit if you can walk outside. Being among nature and out of your same, tired environment allows you to decompress and refocus. It gives you an almost transcendental time to process the overwhelming inputs in a more organized and less emotionally charged manner. If I get into any sort of confrontation, one of the first things I will do is walk outside. I feel more centered, thoughtful, and prepared to address the issue responsibly after giving myself time to decompress. Walking doesn't have to be an all-or-nothing venture. Start slowly, and see if building that routine is feasible. The trickiest part is getting started, but once you do, you experience a positive feedback loop: The more you do it, the more positive effects you'll experience. Make the walk enjoyable with comfortable shoes and possibly someone else to walk with (that way you can dip into social self-care as well!). Vary your routine and location so you are benefiting from the dopamine release of new stimuli around you. And don't stress about skipping days. The emphasis should be on how good you feel when you dedicate that time to yourself instead of penalizing yourself for breaking routine.

Walking offers the physical benefits of exercise while boosting your emotional well-being and helping you gain autonomy over your ADHD symptoms. So, take five, grab your shoes, and get walking!

Try a Headstand

I know this sounds weird.

A headstand requires you to turn your body upside down and stand on your hands. Turns out this is a profound isometric exercise that helps in the consolidation of one's core strength. It also helps regulate blood perfusion and lymph circulation. But why is that good for people with ADHD?

The time spent in inversion can boost your mood by getting extra blood flow to your brain. Headstands can also reduce the production of cortisol (stress hormone), so you are less likely to feel overwhelmed. For an overactive, overstimulated brain, this is a welcome exercise to help calm things down while simultaneously energizing you.

So put down this book and try a headstand (for a quick little pick-me-up!) Here's how:

1. Start with your face away from the wall, hinge down, and put your palms on the ground in front of you, shoulder-width apart (you may want to do this on carpet or a mat in case things get away from you).

2. Climb your feet up the wall until you are upright.

3. Slowly inch your palms back closer to the wall.

4. Hold this position while you count to fifteen and then find a graceful (or not) way to dismount.

Major bonus points if you can pair this with a breathing exercise (inhale and exhale your way to the "Practice Deep Breathing" entry in Chapter 3).

Maintain Regular Doctor's Visits

So often we treat our bodies with reckless abandon. Sure, I can drink nothing but coffee all day, then have my first meal at 3 p.m. Sure, I can skip exercising for months, then try to hike a mountain on vacation. Sure, I can scroll my phone until 2 a.m., then get up at 6 a.m. for work. But eventually, my body becomes tired of my antics and reaches its limit.

Obviously, I do not recommend doing any of these things. A physician can help course-correct and optimize your schedule, diet, and physical well-being. Keeping in regular contact will help your doctor learn the intricacies of your medical history and guide you toward better symptom management.

This is especially important if you have a family history of chronic illness, if you have had any sudden changes in condition, or if your physical health is strongly impacting your mental state. Building these good working relationships and having a therapeutic team to stay on top of your overall health will help you pursue preventive measures and hopefully stave off any larger problems.

The way you take care of your body directly impacts the way your brain functions. Having an established relationship with a primary care doctor can help ensure that you live a long and healthy life so you can spend your mental energy on passion projects versus googling every physical symptom you may experience.

Modulate Caffeine Intake

Caffeine is a stimulant that works on your central nervous system to boost dopamine production. This has been shown to enhance performance by aiding with attention, boosting memory, and regulating body movement. However, this promotion of alertness can also cause anxiety, rapid heart rate, restlessness, headaches, insomnia, and muscle twitches.

Caffeine is also a vasoconstrictor (something that makes blood vessels constrict and reduces blood flow). One theory is that this vasoconstrictive property may help ADHD symptoms by reducing blood flow to hyperactive regions of the brain, allowing them to operate more effectively and cooperate with the rest of the brain.

For someone with ADHD, caffeine can become a habit, and it's easy to overdo it. If you feel more productive, less lethargic, and overall better with caffeine, it's easy to rely on it and take one or two extra cups of coffee or reach for another energy drink for that quick fix. As this moves from a temporary measure to more of a problematic habit, you may notice that the negative aspects of your ADHD are heightened while overly caffeinated, including more uncomfortable hyperfocus, jitteriness, and forgetfulness.

There is no single best practice when it comes to how you utilize caffeine. For some, it improves attention, and for others, it causes anxiety. The trick is to know how it best suits you. It takes about thirty to sixty minutes for caffeine to reach peak effect and about five hours to fully get out of your system. It is important to know these numbers because if you are using caffeine to aid with a certain task, you can time your intake to fit in that window. It is also good to know when caffeine ceases to have a clinical effect so that you can ensure it does not interfere with sleep. The

Mayo Clinic reports that 400 milligrams (about four cups of coffee) of caffeine each day is safe for an adult. The key is to strike a balance, so you don't get jittery and anxious, but you still feel a benefit from the caffeine.

While studies are not conclusive on caffeine as a treatment for ADHD and it is commonly held that the amount of caffeine you would need to consume to impact ADHD symptoms would probably cause agitation, we still can utilize it as a therapeutic tool to give a boost in those low-dopamine canyons.

Everyone reacts differently, and there is a learning curve, but if you can figure out a way to use caffeine to help you, wouldn't that be something?

How to Modulate Bingeing

Binge eating is characterized by eating large amounts of food in short periods of time (often when a person is not hungry) and can result in guilt and profound shame. This compulsive pattern of eating with ADHD can be attributed to poor self-regulation. When you are bored or upset, your brain may misinterpret those feelings as hunger pangs.

It's not easy to combat something you are not aware of. The key is to modulate how you think and feel to eventually alter your behaviors. Here are some starting points so you can regulate more effectively:

- **Avoid food temptations.** Keep the things you binge on out of the house.

- **Replace your mindless eating.** Instead of focusing on *not* eating, focus on changing what/how much you eat. If you feel particularly strong cravings, instead of just depriving yourself, reduce the portion or look up alternatives with a similar flavor profile.

- **Schedule when you eat.** Steady food intake regulates blood sugar so you can make better choices.

- **Recognize boredom.** Find healthy activities to stimulate yourself so that you don't lean on food for dopamine surges (avoid TV, which just encourages mindless eating).

- **Be mindful while eating.** Ask yourself questions about flavors, textures, and overall experience while eating. It will help keep you engaged and present in the moment.

Make Time for a Shower

Personal hygiene can be an issue for people with ADHD. Among children, it is tolerated to a degree, but an adult's poor hygiene can make them look negligent and be indicative of a deeper issue. This leads to an almost corrosive shame, burning down to your core. It's *not* just you. People just don't talk about it.

People with ADHD generally have difficulties in this sphere because of issues with time perception, lack of motivation and forgetfulness, or significant sensory issues. Maybe you hate the feeling of being wet? Maybe the idea of washing your hair leaves you exhausted before you even start? Maybe you feel like it will take too much time or is just too boring? Being able to put your executive function into action to take care of your personal hygiene may be a persistent struggle.

Setting aside time each day to hopefully cement a habit can be helpful. Generally, the mornings can be chaotic, so you may have more success if you build a hygiene practice into your bedtime routine. This can also function as a way to enhance relaxation as you prepare for sleep. The heat of the water can release dopamine, and that quiet personal time can provide some uninterrupted time to work on emotional regulation.

If this resonates with you, maybe a fun shower playlist would help? I'm thinking anything with "Let's Groove" by Earth, Wind & Fire on it.

Incorporate Good Sleep Hygiene

An estimated 25–50 percent of people with ADHD experience sleep problems, ranging from insomnia to secondary sleep conditions. Sleep problems may be the result of impaired arousal, alertness, and regulation circuits in the brain. Other theories propose that issues can stem from delayed circadian rhythm with a later onset of melatonin production. More research needs to be done, but the bottom line is that sleep dysfunction with ADHD is very common.

When you are operating on a sleep deficit, your brain is not functioning optimally, and it can be hard to initiate or sustain focus, make decisions, or regulate emotions. Sleep deprivation and ADHD symptoms have significant overlap, so it stands to reason that sleep deprivation amplifies ADHD symptoms.

Sleep can be a difficult thing to manage and modulate. Good sleep hygiene is multifaceted and can be a very personalized practice. Some things to consider incorporating into your routine to aid with sleep may be:

- **Shut down electronics about thirty to sixty minutes before bed.** The blue light emanating from electronics activates the brain and prevents that "cool-down" period that precedes sleep. In addition to the background light, whatever you are looking at on the phone or iPad or TV is probably very stimulating, which also keeps your brain spinning instead of sleeping.

- **Use your bed only for sleep** (and sex) so you strengthen its association with sleep. No work or eating or phone calls—I'm looking at *you*.

- **Try as hard as you can to wake up at the same time** (even if you are very tired in the morning) and avoid naps. This will ensure that you are tired at nighttime, which helps regulate a more normal sleep-wake cycle.

- **Try a weighted blanket.** This is commonly used for anxiety disorders and has also been shown to provide a calming sensation through the gentle weight and pressure that help guide you into a peaceful slumber.

- **Create a soothing bedtime ritual** like taking a warm bath, reading something calming and not overly stimulating, drinking warm milk or caffeine-free tea, and/or listening to calming music/sounds. The goal here is to wind down the brain and help create circuitry linking these behaviors to initiate sleep.

The fact is that getting enough sleep is a pivotal source of self-care, because if this issue is not addressed there can be significant long-term effects. Not getting enough sleep or having an aberrant sleep cycle can lead to physical illness, behavioral issues, and mood concerns, and this is even more problematic for people with ADHD than for the general population.

Drink Some Green Tea

Green tea has always been my favorite part of dining at Chinese restaurants. Apart from being delicious and soothing to my palate, I've always enjoyed the ceremony of it. I like picking my tea leaves, I like using intricate porcelain tea sets, and I love that it is a social beverage that *isn't* alcohol. I had been drinking tea for years before I learned about its benefits for ADHD.

To understand the therapeutic value of green tea, you need to know its key component: L-theanine. L-theanine is a free amino acid that aids in providing an "alert yet relaxed" state through its activation of alpha brain waves (the same that are present during meditation!). This, coupled with the caffeine in green tea, can enhance learning and concentration. It is also beneficial in providing relief for anxiety while gently energizing you (which is so nice, considering most things that effectively squash anxiety make you groggy and foggy). I can't think of many products available on the market that can calm the mind while focusing attention without adversely affecting alertness.

L-theanine also promotes relaxation and improves your sleep. Getting adequate sleep has tremendous impacts on mood and focus, but the substance itself aids in reducing stress levels and helps with blood pressure. Green tea is also packed with antioxidants, which can decrease neuro-inflammation (seen in dementia and other types of brain degeneration).

If hot tea isn't for you, try matcha, cold mint green tea, or even green tea ice cream!

Get a Massage

Take stock of how you feel right now. Are you sitting hunched over with bunched-up shoulders, stiff neck, and overstrained eyes? Sitting in your chair in legit gargoyle mode? Okay, me too. The problem with this is that your body stores this muscle tension, and you end up paying for it later. Enter the seemingly most "self-indulgent" self-care item in this book: the massage.

You don't need to go to a top-rated spa and spend a full day soaking and steaming and getting massaged (although that sounds awesome). I do suggest that you listen to your body and find what works to release that tension. You can use a foam roller, do guided massage videos, or scam a friend into helping loosen some of those tight muscles.

Massage has specific benefits for people with ADHD. Massage therapy has been shown to decrease fidgeting, promote good focus, and increase serotonin levels. It also has added benefits of enhancing emotional regulation and aiding with more restful sleep. In general (and not just the ADHD population), you can also see an improvement in breathing capacity, circulation, lymphatic drainage, and headaches.

Have you noticed an improvement in symptoms after a massage? Or are you weirded out having someone touch you? If so, you might want to go the foam roller route instead.

Stop Smoking

This is a no-brainer, right? Sadly, it is not that easy. Let me explain why people (and especially ADHD people) have a hard time putting down their cigarettes. Nicotine reaches the brain very rapidly (it is estimated to be about ten seconds). Initially, you see a brief surge in mood and focus, curbed appetite, and enhanced relaxation. This is all precipitated by nicotine stimulating the release of dopamine in the brain, which is what the ADHD brain craves.

But then your brain wants more of it. Regular use of nicotine shifts your body's tolerance to it, thus leading to nicotine withdrawal, which encourages you to smoke again to avoid the feeling. And then, hello dependency.

While nicotine may have had some limited positives on initiation, now you're hooked. Instead of providing calm and relaxation, it now gradually starts increasing anxiety and muscle tension. People with ADHD might get to the point where they realize the short-term benefits aren't worth the long-term deficits, but they *can't* stop because they need that dopamine boost. So, they just keep smoking.

I'm not going to try to convince you to quit. You do you. But you should know what you have signed up for. I encourage you to think about your relationship with smoking: Why do you do it? When do you do it? Where do you do it? I also want you to think about life without smoking: better health, better focus, more regular moods, *fresh breath*.

Did you know that most cravings only last a few minutes? Seriously. Most people don't know that, so they feel this immediate urge when they first feel the pangs of a craving. If you can get past that initial window, you'll be in a physiologically better place to gradually stop altogether.

In just twenty minutes after your last cigarette, your heart rate slows back down. Twelve hours later, levels of carbon monoxide (a toxic gas that *replaces* your precious oxygen) in your blood return to normal. Your lung function improves, and your circulation starts to normalize within three short months. After a year of cessation, your risk of having a heart attack drops by *half*. And after five to fifteen years, your risk of stroke will be the same as that of a nonsmoker.

Quitting is hard. I know a lot of people want to quit but feel like they are "too far in." If you feel like you are having a difficult time knowing where to start or feel like you don't have adequate support to quit, talk to your doctor.

Get an Appropriate Amount of Sunlight

Did you know that sunlight boosts your mood? Sunlight boosts and stimulates the neurochemical serotonin that enhances satisfaction and calmness. Many antidepressants work through the same neurotransmitter to improve mood. You may have also heard about the correlation between sunlight and seasonal affective disorder (SAD). Light therapy boosts the depressive mood precipitated by seasonal change. One study showed that people had higher serotonin levels on sunny days versus cloudy days (independent of the temperature—we are talking just straight sunshine!). A lot more research needs to go into this because there is some confounding data, but it is pretty much universally accepted that we should enjoy that warm sun when we can.

Sunlight appears to play a role in decreasing ADHD symptoms, mostly by promoting good, happy health! It may not have an immediate mood-boosting quality, but by getting out and about in the sun, your mood may incrementally improve, which promotes more restorative sleep, enhanced vitamin D production, and more appropriate mood control.

So do this right now: Peek outside. If it looks sunny, then take a little break and walk around. It can be a two-minute excursion, but really use that time for yourself. Try to check in with your five senses (what do I see, smell, hear, taste, and feel?) when you are outside. This can be a beautiful way to ground yourself, recharge away from fluorescent lights, and soak up some of that solar energy.

Manage Sensory Overload

If you ask me to focus and there are distractions like foot tapping, chewing sounds, dripping, buzzing from a fan, I will be figuring out how to find quiet before I can do anything else. My brain is running on max capacity as it is, and throwing in sensory triggers makes it nearly impossible to keep my focus. The most frustrating part? While these triggers are rendering me incapacitated, everyone else seems to be unbothered!

Sensory-processing problems impact the way you respond to daily events due to impairments in detection, regulation, and interpretation of stimuli. They are more common among the ADHD population. Sometimes sensory dysregulation can almost feel like you are being assaulted by the stimuli and, at other times, like you are fighting for stimulation because you feel like everything is muted. For people with sensory processing issues, things that are not on anyone else's radar can cause extreme discomfort.

It is important to identify what is causing that sensory overload and find a creative solution to cope with it. Some people enlist the help of a physician or occupational therapist to help slowly break them out of these strong sensory patterns. If noises are overstimulating, you may want to try noise-canceling headphones. If tags sewn into your clothing are too much, investigate tagless options or remove the tags. If certain foods are texturally a nightmare, find an alternative way to prepare them.

This isn't just a "you" thing; sensory overload happens to many of us. What things drive you absolutely bananas?

Have a Healthy Relationship with Sex

Sexual stimulation releases endorphins and mobilizes the brain's neurotransmitters. This can calm down the restless feelings that ADHD can cause and provide a brief, blissful break in your brain's constant spinning.

However, there are a lot of potential pitfalls when it comes to sexual behavior and ADHD, and these honestly aren't talked about enough. People with ADHD can experience trouble concentrating during sex, thus making it less enjoyable for the people involved. Another big one is losing interest in a sexual partner. The ADHD brain is wired to chase excitement. As a relationship matures, you may notice that the sparks (dopamine rush!) have subsided, and your brain may try to tell you to move on to something or someone more exciting. Related to that, there is also a high likelihood of impulsivity, which can lead to risky sexual behavior or substance abuse, which then lowers inhibitions and can make impulsivity *worse*.

For those of you in long-term relationships, you may notice sex is less interesting to you because your ADHD has caused a seismic shift in the dynamics of your relationship. Over time, you and your partner may have fallen into a pattern in which your partner has taken on a parental role (and has been forced to take on a majority of the tasks of the home), and you may be shifted into the role of a child (who is being nagged and harangued for your failures). No one wants to have sex in that weird dynamic—it's just rife with possibilities for resentment. Sometimes when this off-putting pattern comes into play, we see people delve almost obsessively into pornography or other self-stimulating methods, which further push them away from building intimacy in a relationship.

Acknowledging aberrant patterns (like the parent/child scenario) can help you rectify the underlying problem. Be mindful, present, and patient as you navigate these waters. Fall back on situations that release dopamine: fun dates, spontaneous adventures, or even things as simple as sweet text messages throughout the day. As you start to let go of resentments and rebalance your relationship, you may notice romance reawakening.

Perhaps the most important step in resolving these frustrating sexual quagmires is to understand that ADHD plays a major role in how you relate to your partner sexually. We often start to make assumptions about our self-worth and desirability based on our partner's views toward us. Acknowledging that this might have nothing to do with you or the love you share and that it's just ADHD symptoms getting in the way of meaningful connection is a fundamental mindset shift that may be necessary to preserve your relationship.

It's important to recognize these patterns because sex is a beautiful way of building intimacy and connection. You should be open with your partners (and yourself) about developing a happy and satisfying sexual relationship.

Curtail Alcohol Use

People with ADHD commonly seek a way to "come down" and calm their brains down. Alcohol sends inhibitory signals to your body telling you to relax, which can be great but also might be problematic if you rely on it to slow down.

While ADHD doesn't cause alcohol misuse, it *is* a risk factor for it. There is data showing that childhood ADHD is associated with earlier alcohol use. There is also a correlation between ADHD and a heightened risk of binge drinking (which may develop into a more chronic alcohol use disorder) and increased sensitivity to alcohol's effects. Perhaps the most important thing to note is that alcohol use could exacerbate symptoms of ADHD, especially impulsivity.

To curtail alcohol use, start by paying attention to the times when it could potentially be most problematic. Avoid drinking alcohol right before bed. It may help you fall asleep, but it interferes with the quality of sleep, meaning you don't progress into a deep sleep and may be more likely to wake up throughout the night or wake up without feeling refreshed. Also, there can be a significant interaction between alcohol and medications. If you are taking a medication, make sure you ask your physician specifically about the interaction with alcohol. Best practice, however, is to avoid alcohol use while the medication is active in your system.

Learn How to Nourish Your Brain

Let's start by debunking some myths about ADHD and food. Unhealthy foods cannot *cause* ADHD. Alternatively, healthy foods cannot *fix* ADHD. What is not a myth is that a poor diet can exacerbate symptoms. By making small tweaks in what, when, and how you eat, you may notice significant improvements in ADHD symptoms.

With ADHD, you may have a hard time regulating your food intake, either forgetting to eat or thoughtlessly eating too much. With these inconsistent patterns, it is especially important to be mindful that when you eat you are making appropriate food choices.

To optimize nutrition and create a diet to best manage your ADHD symptoms, there is evidence to suggest that:

- High-protein diets enhance your ability to initiate and sustain focus, as it takes longer to break down—thus more energy for longer and less crash.

- Complex carbohydrates (whole wheat, quinoa, and so on) versus simple carbohydrates (white bread and sugar) can regulate your supply of energy and promote restful sleep.

- Eating small meals throughout the day can maintain blood sugar levels (fuel for your busy brain!) and enhance overall metabolism.

Eating to properly fuel your body may not come intuitively to people with ADHD, but you can work on making small changes to eventually yield big results. What is one small substitution you can make today?

Work In Good Dental Care

Brushing your teeth can be hard. You know it is the right thing to do, but you literally cannot muster the energy to do it, or you may have sensory issues associated with it, or you just legitimately forget to do it. It can be an embarrassing "failure" to talk about, but it is so common.

ADHD often makes it difficult to pay attention and manage a routine. Cavities are the most common dental issue that dentists see in people with ADHD. It can sometimes be difficult to perform and maintain routine activities like brushing your teeth or flossing, and these poor oral hygiene practices put you at greater risk for cavities. Also, some ADHD medications can dry you out and reduce saliva production, which is necessary to protect teeth.

In a study published by the National Center for Biotechnology Information, only 48 percent of children with ADHD brushed their teeth every morning, and only 48 percent brushed their teeth every evening. Another study showed that children with ADHD were twelve times more likely to have a high number of diseased, missing, and filled teeth.

Something that helped me is to make teeth brushing time a literal dance party. (I even had a Justin Bieber music-playing toothbrush. It was clearly for children.) Find ways to make that mundane task into a dopamine-producing recharge. Finding a routine that works for you is the name of the game.

Dance It Out

I am a miserable dancer. That being said, I love to do it. This made sense when I started to dive into research about the correlation between dance therapy and reduction in ADHD symptoms.

Dance therapy is a wonderful way of managing the more physical side of ADHD. When you think of ADHD, you may think of inattentiveness, hyperactivity, or impulsivity, but somatically, the ADHD body can be tense, dysregulated, and fatigued.

By dancing to your favorite music, you are getting the dopamine rush of an auditory input that you enjoy, as well as positive reinforcement from your physical movements. Dancing allows you to channel energy into something less disruptive, reduces stress, and aids with emotional dysregulation. It also helps with the more traditional facets of focus in ADHD due to increased circulation.

Let's truly revel in the joy of movement. Dance alone, dance with a partner, dance in a group. Connect with your body and take time to appreciate and feel gratitude that you can express yourself in this manner. You may find that while practicing self-awareness and compassion in these episodes of physical release, you may learn to love yourself more. Experiment with different techniques and styles and try to notice afterward if you: Listen better, sleep better, fight less, and feel more fulfilled.

CHAPTER THREE
Mental Self-Care

As a neurodivergent person, you may feel like your brain is always racing with no time to recalibrate and rest. You are expected to perform functions and tasks in the context of a neurotypical world that penalizes your authentic processes and rewards you for masking your symptoms. So how do you take care of your mental health in these circumstances?

Mental self-care includes anything you do to stimulate your mind and nurture a strong and healthy psyche. For ADHD, this form of self-care stems from a deeper understanding of how your brain works. By understanding neurological processes and how to cultivate your lush mental landscape, you can truly begin to take care of yourself.

Practicing mental self-care will help you dampen your internal noise and find ways to better manage stress. The self-care activities in this chapter are meant to help you form healthy habits by working *with* your brain instead of against it. Some of these entries start with some of the basic neurobiological differences in ADHD brains. The hope is that by understanding these fundamentals, you can dive into how to practice the concept of patience, how to cope with feelings of being overwhelmed, and how to find the right therapist to help you navigate better.

Tending to your mental well-being starts from a place of understanding and compassion. It is through those small mindset changes that you start to appreciate more global shifts.

Understand Your Identity

Being repeatedly misunderstood causes people with ADHD to create a false narrative around themselves and their situations. Feeling deficient and not trusting your own brain from an early age makes it extraordinarily difficult to properly evaluate yourself as an adult.

If you have had to endure the criticisms, punishments, and frustrations that accompany ADHD, it can be hard to maintain a positive perception of yourself and your capabilities. Previous experiences and memories of failures or shortcomings come to define your self-identity and suffocate any positive current or past moments. Those lingering words and thoughts fester as you mature and present as an unhealed wound, which informs your decisions moving forward and further perpetuates your emotional dysregulation. You may swing between self-doubt and transiently believing the evidence that you are indeed smart, competent, and capable. It can be exhausting to live this way.

So how do you take back autonomy of your identity and rebuild your narrative?

- **Acknowledge your past.** Dissect and understand your previous experiences that left you feeling misunderstood and see how that translates to current situations. Here's an example: My fourth-grade teacher told me that "if I was really smart, I would have learned how to organize my desk." I now have a clear linkage in my brain of messiness or disorganization meaning that I have failed. That I am dumb. Even today, my heart will sink as I walk past a stack of dirty dishes.

- **Identify your strengths.** Identifying where you excel can help dispel this solely negative narrative. If you're having a hard time doing this and earnestly believing in those strengths, that's what you should be focusing on now.

- **Reframe your memories.** Retell those previous stories and revisit them in a more compassionate way. Although you cannot change that it happened, you can interpret events differently. Going back to my previous example: My fourth-grade teacher thought I wasn't smart because I had a messy desk. I can reframe this by thinking that my teacher might have misunderstood my ADHD symptoms and was trying to say that to motivate me in a way that may have benefited others in the past. There is no correlation between being messy and being smart.

Just remember that you always were and always will be so much more than your ADHD struggle. And I'm sorry if you don't hear that daily, but let's work on telling ourselves that. In your journal or a notebook, write one statement you wish you had heard growing up (to bolster your self-esteem and identity).

Practice Deep Breathing

Do you know how to take a deep breath? I'm being totally serious. A lot of people don't know how to engage their diaphragm during breathing and instead just breathe from their chest or throat.

Try this simple exercise to learn how to do it:

- Sit down and put your hands on your belly.

- Relax the muscles in your neck and shoulders.

- Breathe in slowly through your nose, keeping your mouth closed (I usually count to five).

- Feel your lungs fill with air and inflate like a balloon while your belly moves *outward*. Most people take a deep breath by sucking in their belly. Wrong! Feeling your hands move outward means you are doing it correctly. It kind of takes practice to override the other way.

That's it, you've done it!

But what does deep breathing do for someone with ADHD? This exercise can help you become more attentive and more relaxed at the same time. That appears to be a theoretical paradox, but people with ADHD understand this concept intimately. When your body and brain slow down, you can focus better.

When you can master this breath work, you feel calmer, have better control over your frustration tolerance, and are able to make better decisions. Isn't that wild? And all you have to do is *breathe* properly!

Practice Patience

I have lamentably found that there is a direct correlation between impatience and impulsivity. When I can quell the rising tide of anger, irritability, and exasperation, I find myself accepting and processing data in a more organized manner and am less likely to snap at whoever tries to talk to me next. However, being patient is not something that comes naturally for ADHD brains. It can be difficult to delay instant gratification, and, honestly, we don't do it enough for it to solidify into a habit.

The good news is that patience can be practiced, and the first step is recognizing the situations in which you are impatient. (In conversation? While driving? While eating?) By identifying and understanding the circumstances that automatically kick off that short fuse, you can find ways to prepare yourself ahead of time. Keep in mind that most of the time we become impatient because of poor time management. Perhaps this means reconciling that "time takes time" and removing the pressure of being late by accepting that you get there when you get there. Although striving for promptness is always ideal, in the circumstances when that eludes you, you can shift your mindset to be calm (and late) versus harried and stressed out (and still late).

Trying to slow down and allow time to pass in situations where you are hardwired to accelerate can feel uneasy and foreign. Practice patience in low-stake situations. As you practice, the discomfort will begin to dissipate, and you will become more patient.

Get a Therapist

Learning about the diverse therapy modalities and gaining a deeper understanding of each was an incredibly useful part of my psychiatric training. It was the first time I was able to actually see the benefits of therapy for ADHD symptom management.

Behavioral therapy can help people with ADHD to learn and incorporate skills that manage their symptoms more effectively. The goal of behavioral therapy is to replace negative behaviors with positive ones, thus optimizing your life and creating long-lasting solutions to chronic problems. Behavioral therapy dials down specifically on problem areas like organization, focus, and impulse control.

It is sometimes hard for adults to implement change when there is a weak connection between thoughts and actions. Cognitive behavioral therapy (CBT) may help with that linkage by reframing thoughts to lead to more positive behaviors and thus greater control over ADHD symptoms.

Therapy in ADHD takes an in-depth look at both your difficulties and your triumphs. It helps assess the role ADHD symptoms played in the process. Together with your therapist, you can examine the thoughts, emotions, and behaviors you had during a particular situation. Then you can assess other ways you could have dealt with the situation and build coping techniques to avoid repeating situations. Perhaps the most compelling reason to pursue therapy is that the effects are long-lasting. You are not only processing things in real time; you are also developing the tools to handle roadblocks in the future. Your positive gains continue to grow, and that psychodynamic work becomes further consolidated with time and practice.

Other ways CBT can help in ADHD:

- Coping with negative emotions
- Tracking and understanding behavioral patterns
- Managing stress
- Making time for self-care and self-fulfillment (and finding ways to advocate for this!)
- Shifting self-defeating behaviors
- Resetting negative bias

For me, therapy was especially helpful in my academic training as a resident. I learned skills that aided me with time management, inconsistent motivation, and emotional regulation. It offset the stress of residency, the inevitable depressive lows of defeat, and the circular self-doubt. It was the crucial piece that finally stopped the part of my brain that assigned blame and guilt to every ADHD pitfall I had. I truly feel like therapy, coupled with the loving support of my program directors and peers, got me to a place where I could rebuild my self-esteem and feel inspired to pursue specializing in ADHD patients.

Read a Book

Reading has been a cerebral favorite for years, but did you know that it has distinct properties that make it a formidable form of self-care? Here are some of the top reasons you should indulge your inner bookworm:

- **Stimulates your brain.** Keeping your brain stimulated will lead to more cognitive clarity, intrinsic calmness, and better emotional regulation.

- **Reduces stress.** Fully immersing yourself in a text can therapeutically distract you and help you manage stress in a healthy manner.

- **Provides knowledge.** Gaining information is *always* useful (and can happen quickly if it's something you are naturally interested in).

- **Enhances memory.** Creating new memories helps you forge new synapses (brain pathways) and strengthens existing pathways. This makes your brain fire more effectively and reliably.

- **Allows you to focus longer.** Engaging in the physical act of reading the words and the cognitive act of processing what you are reading helps you sustain focus. The more you do it, the longer those periods get!

Try perusing a bookstore and finding something that really interests you. Then try reading for fifteen minutes before bed and see if you can keep up with the story.

Full disclosure, you may have a hard time going from the high dopamine rushes of flashy Internet content to the placid calmness of words on a page, but it's part of the process. It takes some time to reset.

Create Art

There was a time in my life when I would paint almost every day. It was very therapeutic for me to get all my paints out, pick out my brushes, mix the colors together to build the perfect shade, and then breathe life into a creation that I had been thinking about all day. For people who are creatively wired, this can be extremely restorative. Art therapy utilizes drawing, sculpting, and painting to hone other skills like thoughtful reduction of stress, increased emotional regulation, more controlled physical impulsivity, and mindfulness. Creating art is perhaps most profoundly helpful with boosting self-esteem.

The concept of creating art as a means of expressing emotions has been around since the beginning of time, whether people are aware of it or not. We utilize physical activity and sensory integration and translate our emotional stressors into artwork. As we continue to do so, different parts of our brain light up from engagement (working memory, logic, attention, visual-spatial details).

Simultaneously processing through an emotional weight while creating something inspired releases dopamine, which helps to float you further down this creative pathway. Shortly after this release is enhanced relaxation and reduction in stress levels.

Perhaps the most wonderful thing about art is that it is so personalized. There is no right way to do it. It is just an experience. Find a way to express yourself that feels authentic and healing to you!

Use Social Media Therapeutically

Engaging with social media content can enhance a feeling of being connected to others, but sometimes it can be overwhelming, consuming, and stressful. It is easy to equate your self-worth with how you present on social media and even easier to compare yourself to other people's "perfect" pictures (more about FOMO later!).

Let's discuss how to practice good self-care when it comes to social media.

- **Be aware of hyperfocus** when it comes to scrolling your phone. With ADHD, it can be easy to get sucked into a mindless scroll and lose track of *hours* on content that does not serve you or help you achieve your goals. You may come out of a social media binge and not remember a single post that had an impact. Be mindful of who you follow and make sure the content adds something of value to your life. And try using your phone's time-limit function on certain apps to curtail social media overindulgence.

- **People are not their social media presence.** An easy way to feel inadequate is to compare yourself to these perfectly filtered faces and fun-filled social excursions. These are images and videos specifically curated to look as exciting and glamorous as possible. Remember that comparison is the thief of joy, and social media is *not real life*.

- **Be mindful.** When you are consuming and creating content, it is important to understand your mindset. When you are scrolling, do you feel anxious in the pit of your stomach? Are you jealous? Stressed out? Depressed? It may seem very simple (in retrospect) to put down your phone, but if you are not mindful of what you are doing, you just continue to fester in your discomfort. When you are creating content, are you doing it because you are passionate and engaged or because you wanted to get likes? These are all very plausible driving motivations that you may not be aware of.

- **Don't waste your energy on garbage.** If someone or something makes you feel down or tired or irritable, then block, unfriend, unfollow, or mute. Block and/or report people who post inappropriate or harmful content. There is no reason to allow these images/messages into your private social media bubble. That should be a safe space for you.

And if you still find yourself being significantly impacted, take a social media break. With all the emotionally demanding content out there, taking a break doesn't warrant an explanation other than "it wasn't serving its purpose." You may realize that without the incessant distraction of social media, you are spending more time doing things that are more emotionally fulfilling to you.

Listen to a Podcast

If the thought of listening to something for an hour sends you running for the hills, then this entry is for you. Because that is exactly how I used to feel about podcasts. I never really gave them a chance because the idea of voluntarily giving something my undivided attention seemed impossible.

Podcasts are great for people with ADHD. You can listen to them at your own pace without having to look at anything (a welcome break from staring at rapidly moving images on screens or processing written data). You can pause, rewind, and replay things you missed. You can leave it on in the background while you are cleaning, showering, or stuck in the car.

The recording quality of podcasts is usually pristine, so you're not focusing on background noise, just a single voice or gentle background music. As the podcast continues, you usually get engrossed in the material and find yourself able to sustain your focus until the end.

Some people find that carrying out a monotonous or repetitive task (sorting through laundry, breaking down boxes, unloading the dishwasher) can be a sort of "controlled" fidget and can enhance focus and may help you initiate the focus you need to get through something like a podcast. If you give it a try, and it is still hard to maintain attention, then do something even less mentally activating at the same time (playing with a hairband around your wrist or petting a cat).

Make Your Own Timeline

ADHD can affect your timeline for a lot of things. It is important to understand that the pressure people put on themselves to adhere to strict deadlines for personal milestones may be tolerable to a neurotypical brain, but for people who think differently, it can be stifling. It can repress self-development and force you to rush into things that you are not ready for.

Learning to ignore the nagging presence pushing a time-sensitive agenda can help you achieve real, authentic growth. The key here is that you are making those important life decisions for *you* and not because it is what everyone else is doing. And listen, I know that isn't easy. It isn't comfortable being the one who feels "left behind" while everyone else clips along, but it also isn't easy feeling trapped in a life that isn't your own.

If you're finding yourself on the road less traveled, I want to emphasize the bravery required to take ownership of your own path. It may seem easier to just go with the flow, but it takes real courage to course-correct when you feel that path is too limiting, too permanent, or too poorly timed.

Your timeline is your own timeline. Start school late and finish when you're ready, have babies when you can make room to take care of other humans, or travel where your heart leads you. The speed and order in which you do things are part of *your* personal journey and not anyone else's.

Manage Impostor Syndrome

Impostor syndrome is the phenomenon of doubting your abilities and feeling like a fraud. It involves feelings of incompetence that persist despite your education status, experience, and accomplishments. To cope with these feelings, you might end up working harder than you have to and holding yourself to impossible standards. And it happens a *lot* in people with ADHD.

At the base of impostor syndrome is the conflict between how you perceive yourself versus how others perceive you. It is amplified in ADHD because for years you may have heard you were not doing enough, been told you were not trying the way you should be, and felt like you were consistently falling short. Due to that deep ingraining of self-doubt, you might attribute your successes to good timing and luck rather than skill, hard work, and talent.

You may have worked hard to cloak symptoms and keep parts of yourself hidden, which makes you afraid of people discovering the "real you." You may push yourself to and past your limits to put on a perfect persona to make up for your perceived shortcomings and to reconcile the feeling that you are "tricking" people.

The issue with this is that it becomes a vicious cycle. Any small misstep reinforces your belief in your lack of intelligence and ability. So you work harder. This leads to more errors, which can then drive guilt, shame, anxiety, and depression. You may start to interpret those feelings as positive confirmation that you don't deserve to be where you are.

Here are some strategies to help resolve those contradictory feelings:

- **Acknowledge your feelings.** One of the first things you can do is recognize that it is a possibility that the glowing recognition you are receiving is not from sympathy or pity but because you did a good job. By understanding that there might be some validity to what other people are saying, you take away some of the weight of your own fraudulent feelings.

- **Utilize a neutral sounding board.** This is when a therapist may come in very handy. Share the facts with someone and allow them to provide some context from an outside perspective. Vocalizing your fears to someone else may also help you reframe the situation.

- **Challenge those thoughts.** Is this thought supported by facts, or is this a catastrophic judgment generated by an overactive brain? Look for concrete pieces of evidence versus opinions.

Be your brain's cheerleader. You can accomplish so much, and often it's because of your ability to think differently!

Identify Rejection Sensitivity

Real or perceived rejection is hard for everyone, but it can be paralyzing for people with ADHD. It can keep you from progressing in academic settings, careers, and relationships. Some people describe it as a physical sensation of being "punched in the stomach" or having the air pushed out of your chest. Your body is having a very physiological response to rejection. Even though this isn't part of the diagnostic criteria of ADHD, most people with ADHD experience some form of rejection sensitive dysphoria (RSD).

Learning how to identify when RSD is happening is vital, as it can commonly be mistaken for a mood episode. You may experience some of the following:

- You may have a robust emotional outburst when you feel rejected or criticized.

- You may have social anxiety.

- You may have turbulent relationships and difficulty maintaining healthy communication.

- You may have low self-esteem.

- You may feel like a failure.

The difficult thing about managing RSD is that episodes can happen suddenly and can be very intense. Although some data suggest that certain medications may be helpful, you may only be able to manage things by learning how to handle rejection better. It is impossible to avoid rejection or criticism, but it *is* possible to manage your response so that you handle it more gracefully.

Understand and Recognize Hyperfocus

Hyperfocus is an intense fixation on an interest or activity for an extended period of time. This preoccupation usually happens when you are working on things you are interested in, and it can be so engrossing that you actually block out the world around you.

This phenomenon is thought to stem from low levels of dopamine. Due to this deficit, it is hard to pull yourself out of something you are engaged in to participate in a *less* stimulating task. The ADHD brain is drawn to activities that provide instant gratification.

Hyperfocus can be a wonderful asset. People with this ability can sometimes channel it into something productive, which gives them an advantage over people whose focus dissolves in a much shorter time frame. However, it can also carry its liabilities. If hyperfocus is not funneled the right way, it can lead to academic failure, decreased productivity, and strained relationships.

Understanding and recognizing your hyperfocus is often the first step. Once you recognize that you might slip into hyperfocus, it is vital to use external cues. Some examples are setting alarms, time-usage alerts on the computer, and even asking a partner or coworker to "snap you out of it."

So if you have ever heard "You can't have ADHD, because you can focus on _____ for hours!" well, it's called hyperfocus. It can be wonderful, or it can be highly disruptive, and it's definitely a part of ADHD.

Recognize and Acknowledge Feeling Overwhelmed

How many times have you felt overwhelmed, but you can't articulate exactly what is tipping the scale? How many times have you felt like your head is getting pushed underwater—succumbing to the weight of ten thousand small things? The ADHD brain doesn't effectively filter information or stimulation. As a result of this informational flooding and haphazard organization of stimuli, getting overwhelmed is very common.

A patient once told me that she is "constantly thinking all of the thoughts," and that really resonated with me. What an exhausting process it is to poorly filter salient, meaningful ideas from rapidly passing thoughts. The result of this broken-down system is that you allot similar time and energy to *every* thought, which can be cognitively arduous and consuming.

The overactive brain can also trigger a strong emotional reaction, which activates our already over-responsive nervous system, which results in a tidal wave of inadequately regulated feelings. When you are in this hyperemotional response state, your frontal lobe (in charge of rational processing) is basically offline. It reengages when you slow down a little, but at that moment, the only way to carry yourself through is to *feel* your way through it, which can be miserable.

Here are some tips on how to control the crushing tide of being overwhelmed:

- Notice how you *feel* when you are overwhelmed. Do you have physical symptoms? Headache, stomach cramping, excessive fatigue? Do you have mood changes? Irritability or feeling like you are on the verge of tears? When you recognize your personal signs of being overwhelmed, you can deal with things before you are rendered incapacitated.

- **Take a break.** Move away from whatever is triggering you and change your location. Sometimes just the change in scenery as a way of removing yourself from whatever is triggering you (even if you aren't sure what it is!) can shift you into a more rational place.

- **Breathe through the moment.** When you are overwhelmed, your nervous system lets you know. Suddenly, everything is amplified and chaotic. Deep breathing resets that core and gives your brain enough time and space for your frontal lobe to reengage.

- **Try to figure out what has prompted this feeling.** This part can be difficult because when you are highly overstimulated, it can be difficult to tease out variables. As you become more mindful and know what to look for, this process gets easier.

- **Avoid the blame game.** It is not your *fault* that you are overwhelmed. Your brain is wired to arrive at that location much faster than the average neurotypical person. That's not a moral failing. It is just what you must learn and manage to be successful.

Calm Your Nervous System

The ADHD nervous system is hyperexcitable and rarely at rest. Even when not actively engaged in thought, your nervous system is processing and trying to make sense of external stimuli. It is more sensitive to outside input but poorly filters through it, so you may feel like you respond to *everything*. Sounds can seem louder than normal and may even invoke disgust and rage. Textures could drive you bonkers and limit what you can wear. Certain smells that are faint to everyone else may be overpowering.

It can be exhausting to have your world constantly disrupted by things that don't even land on the neurotypical radar. Here are some ways to quell that neural excitability:

- **Find some space.** Allow your brain to have some space to de-escalate and recalibrate. The goal is to reduce stimulation and maximize the opportunity for relaxation.

- **Add some weight.** Weight, like that from a weighted blanket, provides the brain with input, which can produce a calming and organizing effect on the nervous system.

- **Eat some fat.** Your nervous system is encased in a protective coating that is primarily composed of fats. Eat healthy fats to literally cushion and bolster those frazzled nerves.

For people with ADHD, learning how to mindfully quiet your chaotic neural network can lead to improved symptomatic control and an increased sense of well-being.

Go Into Nature

People who spend more time in nature have an enhanced ability to pay attention and lower levels of stress and anxiety. The research shows that the greater the exposure to nature, the greater your attentiveness.

I think that to understand why nature is so restorative, we must understand the alternative. Our current setting is extremely stimulating. Your attention is constantly being drawn elsewhere, and it is very difficult to engage fully and mindfully in something without feeling like you are ignoring something that needs your attention more. We live in this chronic state of struggling to maintain attention. Eventually, we use up our brain's resources and feel fatigued and depleted. Your brain needs time to recalibrate and "reset," and *that* is what being outside can provide.

People who spend some of their time in nature tend to see a decrease in challenges with short-term memory, hyperactivity, and emotional dysregulation. Their ability to initiate and sustain focus improves. Part of the benefit may be due to organic compounds released by plants, which reduce blood pressure, regulate autonomic activity, and boost immune functioning, all of which can impact the brain's functioning.

I am not suggesting you pack up and spend a week camping at Yosemite, but making small changes to incorporate more nature may be worthwhile modifications. Set up your desk so you can see trees outside, drive the scenic route home, or take a short walk outside before starting something that requires focus.

Find the Humor in ADHD

I love painting, but I really hate cleaning up. Washing off oil paints is *such* an ordeal, and I will almost always leave my paints out with promises that I will clean everything up the next day. One day, my long-haired Himalayan cat Pearl got into said paints. I should preface this story with the fact that my parents loved that cat easily as much as their own children, so Pearl was treated like legit royalty around our house. I was horrified to find him smugly sitting directly on top of my very wet palette. I was even more horrified when I couldn't remove him from the palette because the paint had dried into his fur.

In utter panic, I called our vet, who reluctantly agreed to have the groomer stay to help. I smushed Pearl into his carrier (still firmly affixed to my palette) and rushed to get him to the groomer before my parents came home. I nervously paced until the technician handed me Pearl in his cat carrier. I don't even think I thanked him (much less let him get a word in) in my hurry to zoom back home.

When I got there, my mom was already home. She asked why Pearl was in his carrier, and I responded that I got him groomed as a treat. She was delighted. I was delighted. It wasn't until she opened the case and actually screamed that I discovered what had happened.

Pearl was *totally* shaved, except for his dumb little head. Even poor Pearl knew he looked stupid and was furious about it.

That horrific chain of events was punctuated by points of ADHD breakdown. The way I generally cope with these inevitable moments is *humor*. Humor is a pivotal protective agent from negative self-talk and helps you gain more control of the narrative. We spend such a significant majority of our lives dealing with the destructive stigma and devaluation that come with ADHD, that being able to reframe your thoughts and words around your symptoms may be more beneficial than you think.

Being able to laugh at your mistakes can be important in helping keep things in perspective and reducing the guilt and shame of making mistakes. For ADHD adults who deal with rejection sensitivity and chronic frustration, this may also be a way to deflect some of those unpleasant feelings. This kind of healthy coping around areas of sensitivity can also lead to emotional resiliency, which makes you more likely to attempt challenges and better handle setbacks.

Now, this is not an invitation to be self-deprecating, but if you're in the market to lighten things up, I suggest you crack some jokes, follow some humorous accounts online, or just take a moment to find some comedy in your current situation.

Take a Nap

There are many benefits of napping, but there are potentially even more for people with ADHD. Taking a brief break from the toil of the everyday grind can be soothing, but did you know that it can also improve cognitive function? Speed up reaction time? Help with problem-solving?

Various studies have looked at the correlation between napping and enhanced executive-function abilities. Even a short nap can help slice through sleepiness and fatigue and serve to reinvigorate you. Just taking that neural break from processing external stimuli can better equip you to learn new tasks and commit things to memory more effectively. But besides the cognitive impacts, napping can also aid in emotional regulation. Research has shown that people have a higher threshold for frustration and tend to be less impulsive after a nap.

However, not all naps are created equal. The length of the nap is key to its therapeutic value: too short, and you will not feel refreshed; too long, and you'll sink into deeper stages of sleep that are more difficult to rouse from or that impact your sleep cycle for the night. The magic number is between fifteen and thirty minutes. This is not a daily requirement, but on some days (maybe during that midafternoon slump?), if you are having difficulty being productive, maybe you can use that time to nap?

And if you're one of those people who just can't nap during the day, that's okay too. You don't have to siesta to be at this fiesta.

Utilize Therapeutic Distraction

So much of this book is about how to avoid getting distracted, but what if I told you there was a way to use distraction *therapeutically*? Purposeful use of distraction can be a powerful tool in helping you cope with emotions that are too big to process through in the moment. When ADHD brains are wading through emotional-regulation issues, we sometimes need to distract ourselves as a form of self-care.

You subconsciously do this all the time. When you are thrust into an elevated sense of distress, you seek ways to de-escalate. Therein lies a distinction: What is a negative distraction versus a therapeutic distraction? Often, people try to self-soothe and distract themselves with alcohol and drug use, which may make things seem better temporarily but then inevitably cause rebound feelings of instability and shame. A therapeutic distraction is something that can keep you regulated in the moment and prevent unhealthy coping behaviors. It is a temporary measure until you are in a more level place to process and manage overwhelming emotional data. It is not a means to escape or avoid feeling something; rather, therapeutic distraction gives you control over a situation until there is a better time to cope with it, which invariably yields better outcomes.

The next time something throws your brain into a tailspin, distract yourself in a healthy way until you can deal with it more logically. Clean out your fridge, unsubscribe from emails, or pick your next bingeable TV show. For once, you may be grateful for your ability to distract yourself!

Embrace Thinking Differently

Our brains are wired differently than neurotypical brains. We can be chastised for being mercurial, ineffective, inefficient, and even lazy but also lauded for being creative, spontaneous, energetic, and resourceful. Learning to embrace the nuances of your ADHD symptoms and understanding that there is a neurobiological basis for these differences can be two of the most important things you do on this journey toward self-acceptance.

The primary obstacle to understanding and managing ADHD is trying to force your brain into a world that is not built to accommodate neurodivergence. You are told to assimilate into this dominant culture but are set up for failure because your brain is not wired to flourish under those circumstances. It is only when you accept that you think *differently* that you can achieve your fullest potential.

To start, our understanding of the world is completely different from a neurotypical person's understanding. We have difficulty understanding the concept of past, present, and future, and as a result, it is hard to learn from the mistakes of the past or plan for the consequences of the future. People with ADHD have an unbridled sense of urgency about everything, because if it isn't tackled immediately, it is likely to be forgotten or lost. Instead of being able to prioritize based on importance, we start tasks from what is easiest or most immediately engaging, thus making the rest of the process complicated and occasionally redundant. This is why it can be difficult to commence, continue, and conclude tasks without getting totally overwhelmed.

The way we process external data and interpret it internally is very different as well. People with ADHD tend to feel things more deeply and passionately, which can lead to more robust emotional responses. While someone with ADHD may thrive in a chaotic environment because they can process data quickly, they may find calmer situations overwhelming. We are expected to perform and self-regulate with very little awareness of our mannerisms, actions, and behaviors. It is hard to gauge how we are personally doing, how we are affecting others, and what the subsequent consequences are. People may interpret that as being self-centered or thoughtless because we are not processing their social cues and subtle emotional nuances appropriately. The problem is due to a broken feed-back loop. We cannot see what is going on in real time, so we cannot fix the behavior. If the issue is not corrected, it is reinforced, but this time with an added layer of discomfort and trepidation because we don't know if we are destined to repeat the mistake. This further substantiates the rejection sensitivity that so many of us feel.

Despite those differences, we deserve to celebrate the positives. Our effervescent nature grants us certain latitude that maybe other people aren't afforded. Our brain allows us to be at the forefront of innovative thought, and our unyielding determination propels us toward the finish line. Perhaps we were never meant to fit this mold and should instead create our own.

Unplug from Technology

From the moment we wake up, we are bombarded with technological stimuli. Our life is a frenzied flow from screen to screen with pings and notifications disrupting any attention streak we may initiate. We are held hostage by the idea that this next notification could be of great importance, and so we shatter our focus for meaningless social media updates. Personally, without my phone/laptop/iPad, I feel like it is very difficult to sustain basic functionality.

Isn't that a sad thought? We are now hooked to devices that make it nearly impossible to disengage. We willingly succumb to this information and stimulus barrage because we believe there is no alternative. The issue is that our brains aren't wired to maintain this. The parts of our brain dedicated to sorting through this deluge of information are less proficient than they should be, and so it is hard to discern what is important or not. So we just utilize all our "fuel" and resources sifting through nonsense instead of spending it on worthwhile functions.

So how do you fix this? You unplug.

It doesn't have to be right away or all or none. As an introductory step, delegate your digital activities to certain times instead of letting them bleed through your whole day. As you pull away from this constant connectivity, you may realize how much time and mental energy went into participating in it so habitually. Fill up that unconnected time with hobbies, loved ones, and cultivating creativity.

Treat Yourself Daily

Learning to "treat yo'self" is a brilliant therapeutic principle. The premise is that a "treat" doesn't need to be earned or explained. It is the allowance of a small pleasure just because you want it. By learning to provide these modest indulgences, you further the belief that you are worthy of good things. It fills your dopamine bucket and helps you feel content in your journey forward. The more you learn to give to yourself, the more you can ask from yourself in return.

In stark contrast, in a life without these intermittent indulgences, one can feel dragged down, devalued, and drained. They may not feel like they deserve to take a break or have something they enjoy because they haven't *earned* it. As a result, they get so depleted that they reach for anything for comfort, which often means poor coping skills and broken habits. For people that struggle with impulsivity in the first place, it can be even harder to get back on track after slipping off the wagon.

Treating yourself doesn't have to be a huge financial undertaking or something that requires a significant amount of forward thought. It could be taking a break to look at photographs on your phone, buying fruit from a farmer's market, taking a nap after lunch, or reading celebrity gossip in a warm sun patch.

Find some time in a day filled with rigors and responsibilities to *truly* treat yourself.

Expect Lows after Highs

When you accomplish something that takes a significant amount of your blood, sweat, and tears, the burst of happiness feels euphoric. Just sheer bliss and celebration. It's *such* a good place to be. You'd think the logical consequence would be feeling relief and recharging for your next project? Wrong.

Our brains are confused by this flooding of dopamine that comes with good news and are *hungry* for it when it is gone. It is almost as if you have a withdrawal after this time, and now you are just left feeling incomplete, restless, and anxious. You may also feel some anxiety just with the fact that you felt such profound happiness. It may have been such a departure from your baseline that your brain immediately interpreted that now something is wrong. You may be so convinced that something is off (maybe in the past, bad things have happened when you were doing well) that you spend your time waiting for the other shoe to drop instead of enjoying the moment.

So how do you manage these lows? First, understand that this may be your pattern. By acknowledging that you may have a low after a high, you remove the element of surprise and process through things more effectively. It may also benefit you to reframe things by telling yourself something like "You don't feel low because something is wrong, you feel low because something great just happened and your brain is recovering."

Regardless of the lows, really take time and savor those wonderful highs!

CHAPTER FOUR
Social Self-Care

Human beings need social interaction. This is why prioritizing activities that nurture our relationships with others is vital. People with ADHD tend to go either way on this: They either overpack their schedule with social engagements and then burn out, or they feel overwhelmed and then need to socially isolate. The key to finding the right balance is to engage in social self-care so that you can feel fulfilled without feeling overstretched.

Social self-care involves activities that nurture social relationships. Whether it is through volunteering, participating in hobbies, or just learning how to truly communicate with loved ones, there are many approaches to interacting with others in ways that sustain you.

Most of the ideas in this chapter are built around how to take care of these social networks in the context of the unique challenges that ADHD presents. Some examples include learning how to connect with others in a meaningful way, how to disengage from relationships that may not serve you, and how to recharge yourself through the power of community.

We often regard social interaction as something we "allow" after we complete our responsibilities. However, we may need to reframe this. By finding a way to therapeutically include social self-care, we put ourselves in a position where we can achieve our goals more effectively, completely, and with greater satisfaction.

Find a Like-Minded Community

One of the hardest things about navigating through ADHD is reconciling the feeling of being the "only person in the world to feel like this."

You aren't alone. What you are experiencing is legitimate and difficult, and often what you need most is just the validation that this neural chaos is a shared experience. One of the reasons I got on social media in the first place was to find a home. I wanted to find a community and the support of people who experienced the same things I was going through. I was blown away. The ADHD community is so incredibly powerful and has provided me with a very happy, secure spot to learn and share.

Sharing your experiences with other ADHD adults can slice through that isolation and give you hope that you can succeed alongside this diagnosis. And here's the great thing about online communities: They can be as tailored as you like. You can find social media pages, groups, or forums that discuss broad strokes or dial in to niche topics. There are specialty supports for people who are grappling with finding a name for their symptoms, people who don't have access to a physician and are trying to make behavioral modifications, people searching for the next step after recognizing signs in their child, and infinitely more.

There are even in-person events that can help provide support based on your unique needs. There are programs like Children and Adults with Attention-Deficit/Hyperactivity Disorder (CHADD) that sponsor regional networking and educational events. Schools and colleges can also provide a wealth of information on groups, meetings, and networking opportunities. And if there aren't any, start one! There is such a need for support and an underlying yearning to "find your people" that any group you started would fill up quickly and be such an asset to the community.

Spend Time with a Pet

I have two cats, Hazel and Daphne, and they are the most loyal, loving, and emotionally intuitive animals in the world. I tell people that adopting them settled down my life. Let me tell you why.

People with ADHD have a lot of intrinsic difficulty with managing their time, remaining organized, and feeling overwhelmed. Pets can help you build some structure into your schedule. They eat regularly, they expect walks at certain times, and they need certain bathroom privileges. Incorporating those new parameters makes you more intimately aware of time and adhering to a schedule.

ADHD also often presents as difficulty maintaining focus and hyperactivity. People may sometimes struggle with fidgeting and restlessness. Having a pet encourages you to get out and expend some of that energy with them.

The main reason I will almost always support having a pet is that the amount of love and emotional support you get from a pet is unparalleled. Navigating through ADHD can make you feel isolated. Dealing with years of frustration about being the recipient of repeated rejection and criticism can critically wound your self-esteem. Pets don't care about nuances, or how you did at work, or if you were a little weird at a meeting. They just love you. I can't think of anything more wholesome.

Having a pet is not something that you should undertake until you are ready to provide that animal with a good home. However, if the timing is right, a pet can be a wonderful addition to your life.

Dismantle ADHD Myths

I wish that ADHD was better understood in our world. The problem isn't the lack of information; it is the overwhelming amount of misinformation. When discussing ADHD with friends and family, we are sometimes faced with how to address these inaccuracies in a gentle, nonconfrontational way. Our aim is to feel better understood while using evidence-based information to strengthen our relationships.

Here are a few common myths and some sound bites that can counteract them:

1. **Myth 1: "ADHD isn't real."** Fact: The National Institutes of Health, the Centers for Disease Control and Prevention, and the American Psychiatric Association all recognize ADHD as a medical condition. It is one of the most common conditions in childhood, and most people don't outgrow it.

2. **Myth 2: "People with ADHD aren't able to focus."** Fact: ADHD is more an issue with regulation of focus than a deficit in focus. If people with ADHD are naturally engaged and interested in something, they can focus on it so intently that the rest of the world melts away (hyperfocus).

3. **Myth 3: "You just need to try harder."** Fact: ADHD isn't an inherent problem of motivation or laziness. People with ADHD cannot volitionally override their symptoms through sheer will-power. This is the equivalent of telling someone with glasses to just "see better."

Learn How to Handle Conflict

For the record, I am not the best at handling conflict. Unfortunately, my overstimulated brain sometimes responds erratically or thoughtlessly, and then I spend the rest of the encounter figuring out how to rectify it. Generally, when I am facing something emotionally taxing, I tend to respond emotionally, impulsively, or not at all.

As you could have guessed, those aren't the most effective strategies. Here are some more constructive tips for dealing with a conflict:

- **Ask if this is a good time to talk.** This approach considers the other person's time and mental energy. If they say it is not a good time, respect that, and ask if another time would be better.

- **State your issue in a nonjudgmental fashion.** It is best to be calm, nonthreatening, and emotionally neutral. Practice a few times until you are comfortable with your wording, as this can set the tone of the conversation.

- **Practice active listening.** People with ADHD tend to interrupt and respond impulsively, and this can be heightened in times of emotional overload. Monopolizing the conversation isn't going to resolve the issue and may further the narrative that you are unwilling to listen.

- **Be mindful of your tone.** This is important because when you are dealing with emotional "flooding," you may tend to raise your voice or talk faster as you are getting overstimulated. This is problematic because it signals to the other person that this is an escalating matter, and it starts to move away from a more logical conclusion.

- **Use "I" statements.** Speaking from your own experience and explaining your own emotional state is always preferable to using "you" statements, which can sound accusatory and invalidating.

Most people struggle with resolving conflict, but people with ADHD are particularly impacted by this, because it can be hard to process our own emotions, much less those of others. As a result, we may be unaware of escalating conflict until it's a crisis. Alternatively, we may misinterpret what is happening and then feel like it is the other person's responsibility to resolve the disconnect.

If you relate to this, the most important thing can be to recognize when you start getting overwhelmed. I am (slowly) getting to the point where, if I know I won't be able to handle conflict well, I ask if I can take a break to "process." Usually, my brain stops spinning out of control, and then I can respond rationally. How do you handle conflict: Fight or flight?

Help Educate Others about ADHD

There are about ten million people in the United States with ADHD (and a majority of the adult population with ADHD do not know they have it!). Despite this astounding number, there is a lot of misleading information regarding this diagnosis. This was the initial reason I joined social media: to enhance advocacy regarding the stigma of ADHD but also to provide a safe spot on the Internet where people could access medically sound information.

Using these platforms or other arenas to break down stigma and educate is important. We need more people to reinforce that ADHD is not only real; it is also treatable. We need to educate people that management looks different for every person and learning to utilize self-care and self-compassion is vital.

Being a content generator on social media is not something I ever considered before a year ago. Now, as I am completely immersed in it, I recognize the value of providing research-backed, data-driven information in a palatable, engaging manner. I am more acutely aware of the misconceptions and fears about ADHD, the controversy surrounding it, the limitations of seeking care, and the concerns of stigmatization.

I strongly believe that this is the pathway for those looking to reach a previously obscured population. It could provide them with their first exposure to meaningful information, which could then lead to diagnosis and treatment.

If you do get on social media, look me up @thepsychdoctormd.

Leave Time Between
Commitments to Recalibrate

There is nothing worse than when your brain goes "stagnant"—that inescapable feeling of your mental circuitry running slow laps but unable to reach any reasonable solution. It is a well-known and universally reviled feeling and often is the result of running out of fuel.

Your brain needs time to rest and recharge. Allowing time to recalibrate between commitments gives you time to process data in a relaxed manner, thus allowing you to enter your next challenge with a heightened ability to focus. As you quietly decompress between events, your brain shifts into a lower-consumption mode, and all those extraneous thoughts and inputs can work themselves out rather than showing up later as a poorly timed distraction.

When I'm not cognizant of what my brain needs, I tend to overcommit. I fill my schedule with back-to-back engagements that require different skill sets, thought profiles, and social nuances. I spend a significant amount of neural power transitioning from one event to another. I generally don't give myself any downtime, and only realize it is a problem when I am stuck in that dreaded stagnated state.

Be proactive the next time you are faced with a hectic, cognitively demanding schedule. Make these little breaks a priority. It will ensure that you do your tasks with an enhanced level of attention and allow you to dedicate your mental energy to the things you like, instead of spending your time batting away thoughts that don't serve you in the moment.

Reduce FOMO

FOMO stands for "Fear of Missing Out." It involves two processes: the perception of missing out, followed by the compulsive behaviors to maintain social connections. People have speculated that FOMO stems from the intrinsic need to belong. FOMO has also been thought to be the cause of more negative life experiences (poor sleep, higher anxiety, and feeling a lack of emotional control).

In general, this sounds problematic, but imagine FOMO in a population of people who are already wired to be *rejection sensitive*? It's a disaster.

It is reasonable to speculate that people with ADHD are more vulnerable to FOMO. It is also increasingly hard to process past that phenomenon, as we already have issues with self-evaluation, self-monitoring, and the ability to interpret the impact of social situations.

But what can you do? When FOMO comes your way, remember these five tips:

1. Slow down. ADHD brains are already programmed to whiz by much faster than the average brain. Learn to consciously take your time doing things, so you are not just constantly living in search of the next activity.

2. You can't have it all. Learning to prioritize your needs/wants helps you decide which ones to let go of so you can give appropriate focus and energy to things that are meaningful to you.

3. Understand what is important. Learning to tease out what you want versus what you need is difficult, especially if your brain is *screaming* at you to pick the option of immediate gratification.

4. **Do one thing at a time.** Multitasking doesn't work. When people attempt to apply themselves to too many tasks at once, they have a hard time being effective at completing tasks. When they are focused on a single task, not only are they more likely to be successful; their level of pleasure and fulfillment while performing the task is much higher as well.

5. **Practice gratitude.** By doing this, you more deeply appreciate what you have rather than focusing on what you lack. And if you're looking for tips on how to do that, flip to the "Find What You Are Grateful For" entry in Chapter 1.

FOMO is weird and real, but learning to appreciate your current experience versus lusting after the ones you are missing can promote a heightened sense of personal satisfaction. Here's to living your best life (independently of what anyone else is doing)!

Be Aware of Interrupting

The interrupting struggle is real for people with ADHD. Instead of actively listening to a story, my brain is on fire because I am exploding with the urgency of something that "needs" to be said. And it doesn't stop there. Once I get going, I unleash a lengthy diatribe, which doesn't allow for the other person to interject a single word.

For people with ADHD, interrupting is usually not a volitional act but rather an intricate failure of numerous regulation checkpoints. We may find it difficult to form a thought and then not express it right away due to fearing that we may lose the thought while trying to follow the conversation.

I sincerely wish that I was the person who was heralded as a good listener and able to engage in a generous back-and-forth. The issue is that I am so excited by what you are saying and eager to show understanding that I dysregulate. It is not that I am trying to shut you down or keep you quiet; I just desperately want to be part of the conversation, and, at times, my brain fails to do this delicately.

Often people with ADHD are deemed as being rude or self-absorbed because of this unfortunate phenomenon. Being aware of this might help in social situations or prevent damage in relationships. My tip: When you feel that overwhelming urge to interrupt with a personal anecdote, ask a follow-up question about the other person's story.

Manage TMI

That sinking feeling that you can't "take it back." The immediate energy shift in the room. The inevitable repercussions and sudden unwanted overfamiliarity. Sound familiar?

Oversharing can occur because of impulsivity, an overwhelming emotional state, or the desire to relate to a situation. The downside of this is that sometimes people can regret sharing these overly personal details and feel ashamed or vulnerable. While medication can help slow your zooming brain down, the thing that helps most is recognizing your own patterns.

Here are some things to be mindful of:

- **Don't be too quick to share personal information.** You may feel compelled to join the dialogue with an overly personal anecdote, but it may be hard to understand where to draw the line. If you are able to think before sharing, you may want to ask yourself, would you be okay with this person telling everyone else in the room?

- **If you are overly emotional, give yourself time to cool off.** Often, a verbal deluge is preceded by a state in which your frontal lobe (in charge of judgment) is just flooded with emotional stimuli and cannot process thoughts appropriately.

- **Avoid gossip.** This is a hard one because gossip is generally stimulating, but in these situations, you are prone to get overexcited, overshare, and more than likely damage relationships (or at the very least hurt some feelings).

Cut Out Toxic People

As people with ADHD are more vulnerable to emotional abuse and gaslighting, it is of the utmost importance that you identify toxic people and then take the steps to disengage. It may be readily apparent who is unhealthy for you if they openly and outwardly treat you badly, but there are other people who are toxic in a much more subversive manner. They can cause your self-esteem to plummet and drive you into unhealthy coping mechanisms. They can be quietly manipulative and coerce you into making decisions that you are uncomfortable with. They can stir up chaos in your life surreptitiously and convince you it is a consequence of your ADHD.

One of the most confusing things about these toxic patterns is that you may truly believe this person has your best interests in mind. Perhaps they do, but if the result is that your self-worth suffers, it isn't worth the "intention." You cannot control how other people act, but you can leave if you are not treated the way that you should be.

Here are some ways to pull yourself from the trenches of toxicity:

- Identify what is toxic. Normal, healthy relationships should not persistently make you feel anxious, guilty, or bad about yourself. Ask yourself:
  - Does this person make you feel bad about yourself?
  - Are they your harshest critic?
  - Have they manipulated you?
  - Do they have a hard time controlling their temper?
  - Do they withhold affection frequently?
  - Are they overly self-centered or have a fragile ego?
  - Are they controlling?
  - Do they demand things that make you uncomfortable?

- **Set boundaries.** A toxic person isn't just going to change or cease their behavior when you start to create distance. They may continue to promise change, convince you that this is your fault, or angrily lash out because of a bruised ego. Be firm when setting and maintaining your boundaries for your own mental safety. Do what you need to do to create that space and rebuild your stability.

- **Utilize a support system.** This can be a difficult time to regulate your emotions. It can be scary to navigate through on your own, and the other party may have such a hold on you that it is easy to slide back into old habits without leaning on others for support. Surround yourself with friends, family, and mental health professionals who will be there to help, validate, and plan the next steps forward.

Incorporate Hobbies Into Social Activity

The ADHD brain teems with creativity, energy, and zeal. Whether it is the initial burst of stimulation that comes with leaning into hyperfocus or a tried-and-true hobby that you incorporate into your life, merging your interests with social self-care can be a very rewarding experience.

Finding like-minded people who share your fervor for creative outlets can be affirming and revitalizing. You can find people through support groups, through job/school extracurriculars, or even virtually via social media. Here is a list of suggestions for hobbies that fill your social and dopamine buckets:

- Take an art class. While drawing/painting/sculpting is typically a solo activity, taking a group class can be extremely enriching. Plus, there is the added benefit of growing as an artist by expanding your tastes and techniques by viewing other interpretations of the same assignment.

- Write a screenplay. I was recently speaking with a friend about writing screenplays. Going back and forth, exchanging ideas, drafting, and redrafting can be a beautifully collaborative process.

- Sing in a choir/a capella group. Finding people who enjoy similar music and working together to harmonize *bathes* your brain in dopamine. This may be the perfect melodic answer to restlessness.

Funneling that natural excitability into something you enjoy is wonderful. Getting to share it with others is priceless.

Volunteer for Something Personally Meaningful

Volunteering is an excellent way of taking care of others, but did you know that it can also be a wonderful form of self-care? Research has shown that it positively impacts mental health due to a release of dopamine, which can induce relaxation, reduce anxiety, and quell depression.

Time spent in service of others gives you a sense of purpose, meaning, and appreciation. This is especially true when you spend your time helping in an area you find meaningful. Sometimes the combination of natural interest and the dopamine rush of aiding others is fueled by hyperfocus, and you can create a real, meaningful impact in even a short time.

Volunteering is a great form of social self-care because it helps build a support system of like-minded people with common interests. By participating in a shared activity, you can cultivate new friendships and strengthen existing relationships. Volunteering is a great opportunity to meet new people, expand your social palette, and fine-tune your social skills.

With ADHD, we so often feel lost within our own neural chaos. It is wonderful to find a way to quiet our internal environment while also benefiting our surrounding community. For maximum benefit, find an avenue that you are personally passionate about. Check with nonprofit and cultural organizations, schools, faith communities, or hospitals for options.

And if you need yet another reason to volunteer, individuals who volunteer for selfless reasons live longer than those who do not, according to a study published in *Health Psychology*.

Communicate in Relationships

Navigating through a relationship in which one or more partners has ADHD can be tough. The best piece of advice I have (as someone who has ADHD and as a physician who treats it) is to *talk about it*. Open that dialogue because if you don't discuss your issues, you leave a lot of room for hurt feelings, resentment, and emotional distance.

If you are the person with ADHD in the relationship, you may feel criticized (which we are already exceptionally sensitive to), harangued within an inch of your life, and like you are being treated like a child. This reduces the desire to communicate meaningfully, so you either avoid the other person or just say anything so they stop nagging you. On the flip side, if you are the non-ADHD person in the relationship, you may feel resentful, neglected, and taken advantage of. You may be tired of being the one who does all the logistical parts of daily life and feel like you can't rely on your partner to help ease the burden.

Often, we find ourselves at an impasse of a communication breakdown. Here are some helpful tips to reengage and expand your ability to connect with your partner:

- **Understand when it is the right time to communicate.** Understand where you and your partner are emotionally. One or both of you may need time to emotionally defuse before reengaging in a meaningful way.

- **Figure out the most effective way to convey information.** Sometimes the impasse occurs because one person gets emotional, and the other person shuts down. You cannot communicate effectively if you cannot process the information. Addressing things in a different way, like via email or text, may be a more proficient way of expressing yourself (an added benefit is that it allows you to draft exactly what you want to say). Alternatively, some people need that face-to-face interaction because they get lost in trying to decipher the meaning behind the words without tonal and nonverbal cues.

- Actively listen. One of the most aggravating things for anyone to experience is the perception that their partner is not listening. It's wildly infuriating because it appears that you cannot even validate what they are saying by paying attention. Make good eye contact, affirm and reiterate salient points, and *try* not to interrupt.

Learning how to communicate can lead to a happy, healthy partnership. By discussing and being open about certain behaviors and actions, you can find productive means of addressing these challenges. In the end (with the help of good communication), you may find that the things that were ripping apart your relationship initially were actually the catalyst to bring you closer together.

Cultivate Friendships

My friends are a select group of the most loyal, emotionally intuitive, and endlessly supportive people in the world. However, their best collective quality is being patient. People with ADHD may love the social interaction and support they receive from friendships but have difficulty maintaining these relationships over time.

Progressing through relationships involves making social commitments, reciprocating in communication (and not just forgetting to respond), and navigating through social fatigue. It can seem like hard work, but you are also gaining the benefits of finding a like-minded soul who strives to understand and reassure you. Focus on fostering deep and meaningful relationships in which you can connect authentically, rather than just surrounding yourself with shallow acquaintances (quality over quantity!).

Creating and cultivating these friendships may require some effort. You may struggle in a social gathering to actively listen. You may feel restless and want to jump to another social interaction. You may feel like remembering to keep in touch is yet another thing on your plate. To participate in these relationships, you must make a conscious effort to stay in touch and schedule efforts to reconnect. While it may not seem like a priority, having this wraparound network of friends can encourage, protect, and support you when you need it most.

It doesn't have to be an elaborate event. Call or text a friend. Invite them to participate in an activity that you would be doing anyway. Grab a meal and catch up.

Learn to Say Sorry

The stomach drop when you have said or done something that wasn't right. The slow festering of guilt and anger (not necessarily at the other person, but perhaps at yourself). The surge of nausea, elevated heart rate, and facial flushing when you're dealing with acute embarrassment coupled with shame. These are feelings that you may be all too familiar with as someone with ADHD.

At times, you may be reluctant to initiate an apology. Pride may get in the way. You may feel like you are exposing yourself to vulnerability or humiliation, or even losing a piece of yourself by admitting your fault. At times, you may not even know what you did wrong, but you can piece together the nonverbal cues (folded arms, pursed lips, furrowed brows). Play back the conversation in your head and look for anything that could have caused that appreciable energy shift. Ask friends who may have been there if there was something that you missed.

There are certain therapeutic benefits of apologizing. It quells the feelings of self-reproach. It dampens the visceral physical response to guilt. It can be a humbling experience for the apologizer and restore trust in a relationship for the recipient of the apology. As you explore how to maneuver these opportunities, you can also pride yourself on being able to cultivate courage.

Learning to say sorry can prevent a misunderstanding from turning into an irreversible rift. Take ownership, be sincere, and try to do it sooner rather than later.

Don't Gatekeep the Diagnosis

If you have ADHD, you're most likely going to have to listen to people say things like "Oh, I do that too" when you feel like it is clear as day that they do *not* have ADHD. That's annoying. It took me a long while not to erupt into magma when things like that happened.

But...maybe they *are* experiencing similar things. Who are we to be gatekeepers of other people's symptoms? By "gatekeeping," I mean the act of limiting someone's access to something because they don't look or seem like they meet certain criteria. (A non-mental health example still haunts me: "You can't really be a Smashing Pumpkins fan because you don't own their CD." No, *Emily*. I am a huge fan; I just wasn't *allowed* to get their CD because I'm a fourth grader.) Gatekeeping in mental health can snowball rapidly.

One of the first steps for a lot of people navigating through ADHD is to talk about it with others. Comments such as "That can't be ADHD because that's not what I have" or "You're acing school, so it can't be ADHD" invalidate a person's experiences and possibly discourage them from getting some much-needed help. Side note: This is part of the reason I have a beef with many social media comments. By gatekeeping, we set unrealistic standards based on our personal experiences and our own skewed view of what ADHD should look like.

ADHD can present differently depending on your gender, age, underlying psychiatric conditions, genetics, and a litany of other variables. There is no single way to experience ADHD symptoms, and it is certainly not a competition. If someone falls on the more severe end of the spectrum, that doesn't diminish your own symptomology. On the flip side, if someone is exhibiting a milder presentation, it is not your job to say their symptoms are not valid just because they don't mirror your own experience. If reading this is bothering you, really look into where that anger is coming from. Is it from a place of fear or resources? Is it from a loss of attention on you? Is it from feeling invalidated?

When faced with a situation that I desperately want to gatekeep, I try to reframe things. Instead of explaining why my symptoms are "real" and theirs are not, I ask them what they are doing to cope or who they see to manage their symptoms.

Have you been on either side of the gatekeeping issue? Have you ever wanted to gatekeep, or have you been shut down by gatekeeping?

Create a Self-Care Culture in Your Circle

If we were left to deal with our ADHD in a vacuum, I believe the outcome could be better. We wouldn't have to deal with the judgment, grief and bereavement, and rejection sensitivity that come with interacting with others. We wouldn't have to fight to validate our condition or grapple with the comparisons to the neurotypical state of being. However, complete isolation is not realistic, so instead, you should spend your time creating a self-care culture in your circle, so people are delicate with this diagnosis and do things to uplift you rather than diminish your incandescence.

Research has shown that the most effective way to deal with stigma is to know someone with the disorder who is stigmatized. If we can be comfortable saying to others, "I have ADHD," that usually opens the door for some real and productive dialogue. Encourage others to ask questions. Provide a safe space for them to explore if they exhibit symptoms. Educate them about possible avenues of management and treatment.

Once we achieve a mutual understanding of this neurological disorder, we can work on creating an environment that supports growth. Talk to your family and friends about behavioral techniques you have found that help you manage symptoms and see if they may be receptive to incorporating some of those changes. An example might be: "Sometimes I need to decompress between social events. It really helps me reset and keeps me engaged in the next setting. You should try to call me when you're rested."

Explain ADHD to Loved Ones

It is important to acknowledge and gently educate your surrounding circle about neurobiology and genetic linkage to help them understand ADHD as a medical disorder rather than as a collection of shortcomings. Such efforts may still fall on deaf ears if people are just not ready to hear them.

It is no surprise that people with ADHD have low self-worth when they often have to put up with almost persistent invalidation. Having to explain or argue that what you're feeling is legitimate and medically explainable can be exhausting. Totally exhausting.

Just remember: Your treatment journey is between you and your physician. People will have opinions that may not align with yours, and that's okay. Your priority is *your* health.

But in case you still have to deal with *that* person who wants to give you unsolicited advice, here are some responses you can try:

- Based on my clinical symptoms, that is what the doctor suggested.

- I want to make sure I have every opportunity available so that I can succeed.

- This was my decision and not an invitation for your opinion. (This one is my favorite! SHUT IT DOWN!)

Do you have other ideas about ways to respond to invalidating comments or simply unhelpful "advice"?

Maneuver Difficult Conversations

I will almost always ghost someone rather than have a difficult conversation. I recognize how wildly irresponsible and immature that is. As a person who has been on the receiving end of the ghosting, you would assume that I recognize the unbelievable amount of emotional invalidation that it causes, but...

Having difficult conversations is...difficult. Especially for people with ADHD. You anticipate the criticism and rejection, you catastrophize worst-case scenarios, and you ruminate on past mistakes that led up to this moment. For people with a limited capacity to emotionally regulate, it can be a minefield.

Let's first understand why these situations are so challenging for people with ADHD. People with ADHD may have a hard time dealing with and processing data in real time and have a hard time retrieving valid counterpoints. They may also have to deal with external distractions that keep them from attending fully to the conversation and make it difficult to reciprocate effectively. Due to their emotional-regulation issues, a seemingly innocuous comment can be misinterpreted and set off a fiery cascade, which rapidly devolves conversation into conflict.

This escalated internal tension (attributed to perceived or real reasons) may change how you communicate. Instead of relaying your points in a clear, concise way, you may:

- Get emotionally overwhelmed and shut down
- Respond impulsively or inappropriately
- Become hyperverbal and inarticulate ("just talking in circles")
- Become frustrated and lash out

So how do you bypass these pitfalls?

- **Plan what you want to say.** You may not have this opportunity every time, but when you do have some time to think beforehand, make a list of bullet points and practice them. The purpose of summarizing in this way is to cement the most important things to you and achieve a certain objective. Often with ADHD, you can lose sight of both of these goals because you get caught in the fray and roped into the frivolous fisticuffs of the details.

- **Recognize what your body is telling you.** Sometimes it is hard to nail down what emotion you are feeling, apart from "I'm uncomfortable." Understanding your body cues can help you pinpoint management techniques so you are calmer in the moment and able to attend more completely (for example, the uneasy stomach flip that accompanies anxiety may be a sign to pause and breathe deeply).

- **Be aware of cognitive distortions.** Your brain absolutely wants to play tricks on you. It will distort and misinterpret things that you are hearing to fit the narrative that you are emotionally feeling. Sneaky. Learn to challenge yourself in the moment: Could I be misinterpreting things? Is my perspective valid? If I told this to someone else, would they agree about the tone?

Recognize Self-Sabotage in Relationships

Let's process this: Our brains want dopamine. We get that from stimulation. Is there anything more stimulating in a relationship than falling in love and fighting? When those types of stimulation are "done," the brain is left trying to find a reason for why you are not getting that chemical surge anymore, and then you try to problem-solve when there really isn't a problem. Messy.

People with ADHD are more susceptible to falling victim to emotional abuse and gaslighting. Reasons for why this occurs include poor judgment in picking partners, not trusting their own internal dialogue, previous trauma, or vulnerability from low self-esteem.

Knowing these two pieces of information, that your brain is hardwired to seek out stimulation and that you are predisposed to enter unhealthy relationships, you need to proceed with caution. When looking at a relationship, it is important to gauge whether or not the decisions you are making are driven by your desire for dopamine. Neglecting to attribute that driving urge can result in a few potential outcomes: You leave because you tire of falling into a stable pattern, or you stay in a chaotic environment because you are addicted to the stimulation of the turmoil.

Ask yourself this: "Why do I think something is wrong with my relationship?" If your answers are hard to put your finger on and circle around "I'm bored," it *may* not be an issue with the relationship but rather that you settled into a stable situation without the constant flooding of dopamine.

Become Aware of "People Pleasing"

People with ADHD have a deep sensitivity to emotional pain (learn more about rejection sensitive dysphoria in the "Identify Rejection Sensitivity" entry in Chapter 3), so they may fall into a people-pleasing pattern of always making sure their surrounding circle approves of them. Over time, that person may lose track of their own inherent wants and needs.

It's not necessarily a bad thing to seek approval, but when it leads to the inability to be authentic or a preoccupation with tending to other people's needs as a way of maintaining relationships, you need to reassess the situation.

Here are some signs that you've fallen into a people-pleasing pattern:

- You have a hard time saying no and feel guilty when you do manage to say no.

- You are preoccupied with what other people might think if you say no.

- You agree to things you don't like or do things you don't want to do.

- You want people to like you and feel that doing things for them will help your relationship.

- You're always telling people you're sorry.

- You neglect your own needs to do things for others.

I'm still trying to navigate out of this pattern. I don't want to be perceived as "mean" or "unaccommodating," but in the past, that has always meant pushing myself to the side. Now I try to remain mindful to see why I am saying yes to things.

CHAPTER FIVE

Career/Professional Self-Care

Having to navigate the professional landscape while managing ADHD can seem very difficult. Due to self-worth issues, you may settle for a job that doesn't challenge you intellectually and feel like you are just treading water. On the flip side, due to the fear of being perceived as "lazy," you may push yourself excessively and experience burnout. Finding a healthy medium can be difficult, but this chapter addresses the activities and actions that support feeling balanced and satisfied in your professional career.

ADHD comes with specific characteristics that may make some jobs more suitable for individuals than others. We thrive in situations that require high energy, creativity, and flexibility. While we typically fixate on the negatives of ADHD, it also has positives that make us competitive candidates in a professional setting. We tend to tackle problems creatively, are socially engaging, and can capitalize on waves of hyperfocus. These are all highly desired qualities in employees.

In this chapter, you will find topics that specifically cater to building a work environment that cultivates those positive attributes. We discuss when—or if—to disclose your ADHD, what accommodations you can legally ask for, and how to deal with the grind (paperwork, procrastination, and restlessness). Supporting and strengthening your professional identity will help you gain aptitude and confidence in your field and in a way that you feel engaged and motivated to continue.

Learn to Say No

One of the hardest things to accept about myself is my inability to say no. (Did you read the "Become Aware of 'People Pleasing'" entry in Chapter 4 yet?) If safety or medical issues are involved, I can set boundaries because I have science to back it up, but when it comes to setting boundaries for myself? Forget about it.

But there are *very real* reasons you and I need to work on these issues in order to be better advocates for ourselves. If you constantly say yes to things, you can fall into a pattern where you feel used and become resentful. You can get overwhelmed, causing a self-fulfilling prophecy of failure. And, often, you can just burn out.

Here are some tips to help you *Just Say No*:

- **Establish clear boundaries.** Know where your line is and then vocalize that to others. This doesn't have to be confrontational but can be achieved in small steps, like setting a time when you stop responding to emails.

- **Start with small changes.** Shifting your behavioral patterns all at once would be extremely difficult and may be perceived as erratic by the people around you. Slowly learn to teach yourself (and the people around you!) how to understand your boundaries. A great example of this is to start with voicing your opinion about something small. As you get more comfortable with expressing your needs, you can start utilizing it on bigger things.

- **Know your priorities.** Sometimes we get mired in the pattern of saying yes to everything, then lose time/focus for things we really need to attend to. Saying yes to things that will help you accomplish your goals (and, on the flip side, saying no to things that may not serve you) will help conserve your physical and emotional energy so you can devote that to what is important to you.

- Stall! Immediately agreeing to a task (as so many of us do by default) can leave you feeling overwhelmed. Taking some time to assess the request will ensure that you can decide whether it is reasonable and if you could accomplish it without stressing yourself out. An example is that email that comes in at 4:59 p.m. on a Friday. Instead of rushing to answer it, you can respond by saying, "I want to make sure I have adequate time to assess this request, so I will circle back on Monday."

Remember this, learning to say no is not something you are going to be able to do right away. If you start to feel overwhelmed or tempted to give the "easy yes," remind yourself why you are putting someone else's needs before your own. You deserve to accomplish your own goals, enjoy your own time, and protect your own joy.

Use Your PTO

People with ADHD are often chastised for not being "hard workers," but they can very likely tilt the other way. To compensate for some of their perceived deficits, they overwork and generally pull away from resources in place to take care of themselves. They will often shorten, delay, or cancel their vacation time because they don't feel like it is *deserved*. That mindset is a one-way road to burnout.

A recent study by the World Health Organization (WHO) found that 745,000 people died in 2016 from heart disease and stroke due to long hours and that numbers were continuing to trend upward. The research found that working more than fifty-five hours a week was associated with a 35 percent higher risk of stroke and a 17 percent higher risk of dying from heart disease compared to a workweek of thirty-five to forty hours. Taking time off is vital.

Utilizing your paid time off (PTO) is a simple way to reset. It promotes your professional self-care by increasing enhanced productivity and better performance. Changing locations and environments helps you feel more present and stimulated (and helps break that cursed cycle of boredom). It also helps regulate stress and anxiety, which allows you to think more clearly and process more effectively. Taking that time off can help recalibrate your sleep patterns into something healthier and also improve your capacity to learn, form connections, and make creative decisions. If you are struggling with whether or not you deserve time off, perhaps reframe how you look at it. Instead of whether or not you "deserve" it, you can think of it as vital time to decompress and recharge so that you can engage more fully.

I don't really know what you're waiting for. Put in that vacation request.

List Career Goals

No matter where you are on your professional journey, it is beneficial to set career goals. With the brilliant exuberance of an ADHD brain, we can have big dreams and goals but no tangible route to get there. By listing and breaking down your plans, you are more likely to manifest opportunities that are aligned with your professional path.

Articulating your career aspirations provides a starting point toward the eventual goal. You don't necessarily have to focus on a certain position or financial status. You could concentrate on skill sets you are hoping to develop, like working toward licensure or accreditation in a particular field or specialized training or experiences that help you gain exposure.

This is especially important when you want to switch careers or progress up the ranks. Sharing where you want to go can help you and a potential employer decide if the position is the right fit, or if you can at least consider it an appropriate stepping-stone. And while these "goals" may change as career paths shift and life inevitably gets in the way, having some sort of endgame helps you continue to strive for the dopamine rush of accomplishment on the way.

Being able to pin down your career goals and track the progress you've made in achieving them not only helps you keep that forward momentum; it also keeps you more assured and confident in your professional career.

Learn to Actively Listen

As we have mentioned, ADHD is *not* a deficit of attention. It is a problem *regulating* your attention. You are perfectly capable of focusing, but sometimes it is hard to funnel your attention into what you need focus for, especially if you are not naturally engaged by it.

Thus, you can surmise that actively listening may pose a special challenge for people with ADHD. Part of the issue is that we think faster than others can talk. Then we must deal with our brains trying to fill up those spaces with our own thoughts. It becomes very difficult to participate meaningfully when you are attempting to block out external distractions, table internal thoughts, stave off verbal impulsivity, and maintain interest in a conversation.

It takes a fair amount of energy to process and interpret that auditory data, but becoming a better listener is rewarding for numerous reasons. Being able to engage and actively listen helps you build trust and strengthen relationships, make better decisions more efficiently, and decrease your stress and tension.

Here are my absolute best secret weapons for enhancing your focus and boosting your ability to follow instructions (no matter how boring they may seem!).

- Write it down. Either take notes or ask the person giving the instructions to send you an email/outline/agenda. You may find that writing while someone is verbally providing information promotes active listening and enhances comprehension. Added bonus: You look eager and attentive, and people are into that.

- **Repeat it back.** Echo what was said to make sure you heard it correctly. The additional benefit of this is that it gives you another opportunity to process and commit things to memory.

- **Fidget if you have to.** Sometimes that internal (and external) restlessness prevents you from listening fully. You may be so fixated on *not* moving that you aren't truly listening to what they are saying. Find something that works for you and that isn't disruptive while you are listening: Squeeze a stress ball, walk as you're talking, surreptitiously stretch. Listen to your body's cues; if it's telling you to move, then do it because otherwise your entire focus is going to be "how do I hide this?"

These might seem like no-brainers, but it's bizarre how many skills we forget to apply in the moment. Like a lot of other self-care mechanisms in this book, active listening gets better with practice.

Find a Body Double

For years, I would assert that I would get more done if I was with someone else. The other person literally didn't need to do anything other than be a physical presence, but I think it made me more accountable for my actions, and, frankly, it was just more fun to have another human around.

For many people with ADHD, having someone present while you tackle tasks makes it more likely that they get done. A body double could be a friend, roommate, parent, or spouse who is willing to just physically *be there* while your brain figures out what its next steps are. And if there is no one around you? No problem! Use FaceTime or *YouTube* or social media body-doubling groups.

When would you use body doubling? That's the great thing; you can use it for anything you find tedious or boring, like something you are anticipating having a hard time starting. You can start to plan these body-doubling sessions, and once it becomes a routine, you get the consistent dopamine rush of getting stuff done.

So, when you think about working and start to make excuses, instead consider the possibility of using a body double. You may find it easier to start, sustain, and complete tasks!

Decide Whether to Disclose ADHD

Should you share your diagnosis? That depends on the culture of your workplace and what accommodations could be made. Not everyone is well versed in the nuances of ADHD, and some people might be concerned that your diagnosis would be problematic at some point. First, it is important to figure out what accommodations, if any, your work can provide.

Secondly, you can request modifications that enhance your performance without disclosing your diagnosis. Could I wear headphones, as I get more work done when it is quiet? Can I come in slightly early to help prepare for the day? Is there something we can change to help me perform more effectively?

If you do decide to share your diagnosis, start with the many positives that make you an asset. Creativity, high energy, and being intrinsically good at problem-solving are some wonderful attributes of ADHD brains that can make you a vital part of a company.

If you do disclose your ADHD, frame things positively. Instead of saying, "It is hard for me to pay attention when..." say something like "I do best when...". Come prepared with well-thought-out suggestions for accommodations and be prepared to explain why they would help you do your job better. You are trying to reinforce that this is not an excuse or a shortcut; this is something to enhance your productivity.

Push Aside Perfectionism

People with ADHD are intensely aware of their shortcomings and often struggle with shame and low confidence because of them. Perfectionism is a consequence of this and is bred from the fear of failing to meet impossibly high standards that you've set for yourself. Personally, I have suffered a great deal with the trials and tribulations caused by my ADHD symptoms and have struggled to find a path through them. I think my need for control coupled with the desire to get things right left me caged in a paralyzingly rigid prison of my own making. If I couldn't do it the way I envisioned, I had failed.

I compared myself to my neurotypical peers and punished myself for not reaching my unreasonable standards. I understand now that there are things I can do as well as, if not better than, my neurotypical counterparts. But there are certain ways in which my brain is simply wired differently, and a comparison would be fundamentally invalid. My perfectionism became my defense mechanism to bolster against life's uncertainties and a way to offset my limitations.

The desire to do things a certain way quickly starts careening down the pathway to obsession. Suddenly, the fear of your weak executive functioning leads to rumination and persistent worry: What if I have already messed this up? What happens when everyone else finds out I messed up? How will I be able to handle the criticism if I can't even think about it now? Now you are doubling down, further cementing things, and rechecking things ten times to make things perfect to ensure that you won't be humiliated.

Perfectionist thinking comes into play at many points of your journey. You may be frozen at the outset because you feel like you cannot start because you will inevitably mess up. The threat of not being able to do something perfectly causes you to avoid it altogether. Alternatively, you may be clipping along and then suddenly hit a rough patch. Then you switch gears and start doing things that you are good at while avoiding what actually needs to be done. This may provide short-term relief, but it increases the likelihood that the task will remain unfinished. At the end of this process, you may also feel like "if it's not completely right, then it must be a failure." This all-or-nothing thinking further feeds into feelings of low self-worth at your lack of productivity.

Instead of fixating on perfect, start to embrace what is real. See the positives of the things you have done instead of focusing on the flaws. Understand that feedback is not an attack or manifestation of failure but a chance for you to grow and better yourself. Build on your tenets of self-compassion to support yourself through periods of discomfort and nurture resilience. Being perfect isn't real life.

Put Your Best Face Forward During Interviews

As people with ADHD, we are constantly thinking about how to minimize our symptomology to fit a neurotypical mold. This comes up when we interview for new positions or think about advancing our careers. Often, we have the ambition and drive but don't know how to execute our vision. Here are some tips on how to prepare for career advancement in a way that *highlights* rather than diminishes your uniqueness:

- Research the role. Having a wealth of knowledge gives you a competitive advantage or helps you decide if you even want the job.

- Write down your accomplishments and strengths. Starting with these positives will guide the conversation.

- Reframe your negatives. Have a dialogue about gaps in training/jobs and positively frame explanations for why you left previous jobs (maybe not "I hated my boss," but "I would benefit from more creative management").

- Actively listen and be mindful of interrupting. Take notes to keep track of your racing thoughts.

- Use nonverbal cues. Keep eye contact, walk and sit with confidence, and be mindful of the tone and volume of your voice.

- Be honest. Embellishing your qualifications may eventually result in unrealistic job expectations and heightened stress in the long run.

- Ask questions. Asking questions shows engagement and interest.

- Practice. This may aid you with sound bites so that you can nail down what you want to convey and how to say it.

Ask for What You Want

Learning how to advocate for yourself is not something a lot of people with ADHD do naturally. I don't know if that is because we spent so much time being shut down through our childhood, developed people-pleasing tendencies as a coping mechanism, or we are terrified of rejection or criticism so we refrain from asking for things. We may think that dimming our light and playing down our needs will avoid conflict, but often those are the preliminary steps down a long road of resentment and dissatisfaction.

Asking for what you want doesn't need to be adversarial or contentious. It doesn't even need to be about big things. It can be about small things that help you gain autonomy. Sometimes we know what we want, and know we must ask for it, but we literally don't have the words to do so. Try a few of these conversation starters:

- "Let me see if I understand..."

- "I think I need some time to process. Do you mind if we talk about this later?"

- "For me to be able to complete this to my standards, I need..."

- "I missed what you said. Could you repeat that?"

- "I need to prioritize this right now."

  What keeps you from asking for what you want?

Learn What Accommodations Are Available

ADHD can shatter your confidence so much that you question if it's even worth it to pursue your career dreams. But instead of changing your dream, maybe think about how to change your management of ADHD. Because if it is properly managed, it is a whole new playing field.

Two federal laws may protect you in the workplace: the Rehabilitation Act of 1973 (RA) and the Americans with Disabilities Act of 1990 (ADA), which includes the ADA Amendments Act of 2008 (ADAAA). The ADA includes ADHD as a recognized disability. In accordance with this act, your employer must be able to provide reasonable accommodations, as long as doing so doesn't create an undue hardship to the business, which most of these accommodations do *not*.

Many people with ADHD in the workplace setting want to request accommodations but may not feel ready to disclose their diagnosis to their employer. In that case, you can request small modifications that may aid productivity (wearing headphones at work, having an office/desk away from central gathering areas, and so on).

Once you've done your research and decided to request accommodations from your employer, it is important to conceptualize what accommodations could be put in place to make your work life more manageable. Try to think about what limitations you are experiencing, what specific job tasks they impact, and what would help reduce or eliminate these problems.

If you have limitations related to executive functioning, you can ask for the following accommodations:

- Work remotely from home
- Adjust method of supervision/feedback (hello, rejection sensitive dysphoria!)
- Using your employee assistance program (EAP) to find a therapist
- Private work area that is quieter and more removed from social areas
- Using noise-cancellation or white-noise headphones
- Taking breaks to walk or just recenter yourself

Create a System for Paperwork

If I am not careful, I get completely enveloped in the chaos of paperwork. My desk will be covered with countless papers of varying priorities in no discernable order (which makes it impossible to locate items or maintain deadlines). It also is an external representation of just how haphazard my own internal organization structure is.

Here are a few tips to make managing the mountain of paperwork a little more doable:

- **Deal with it immediately.** Instead of putting paperwork aside in hopes you will address it later (and then almost immediately losing it), organize it based on priority. I have an open three-segment paper holder with "do today, do tomorrow, do later," and I make sure to deal with and reorganize at the end of the day.

- **Purge unnecessary paperwork.** We are constantly swimming in extraneous or irrelevant paperwork. Don't drown; recycle it.

- **Organize creatively.** Color-code or use labels (I like using logos or stickers with images instead of just the name), and make filing fun again.

- **Delegate if possible.** If you have the luxury of an assistant or someone experienced with certain paperwork systems, utilize them. There is no rule that says you need to do everything on your own, and the most successful people know when to delegate. If you have a hard time with that, I suggest flipping to the "Learn to Delegate" entry in this chapter.

Bypass Analysis Paralysis

Do you waver between "I am overwhelmed by too much information" and "I can't make up my mind"? Have you ever felt like your brain keeps spinning down the same thought pathways without coming to any solution? Have you ever missed an opportunity because you couldn't decide? It's agonizing and very real.

People with ADHD do extremely well at making split-second decisions in crisis situations. It is the day-to-day menial slog, however, that is much more difficult: balancing, considering, and evaluating complex information to make an informed choice.

Analysis paralysis refers to a breakdown in executive function. It can be hard to start things, sustain things, and complete things. That leads to a sense of paralysis, whereby you really want to do something but can't make progress. This can happen when your brain is overwhelmed, especially when combined with the fear of making the wrong decision.

Here are three ways to manage being paralyzed between options:

- **Limit your choices.** Your brain doesn't like being stuck between a multitude of options. Give it two to three options at maximum. (For example, for smaller decisions, opt for the easiest decision and move on. Spending hours agonizing over something relatively trivial seems like a waste.)

- **Set a deadline.** You can allow a certain time until the decision. Your brain works better as the deadline approaches due to the boost of adrenaline provided by the time crunch.

- **Find a quiet place to reflect.** When your brain is overstimulated, you can't make reasonable, rational decisions. Taking time to think in a quiet place can help your brain to relax.

Don't Feel Chained to Conventional Careers

A career is defined as an occupation undertaken for a significant period of a person's life. If you are very discerning about the choices you make (or possibly very lucky), you can end up in a career that celebrates who you are, instead of stifling your individuality.

For many people with ADHD, the academic path can be overly strenuous or out of reach. Due to the limitations caused by not attaining a particular academic degree, coupled with the paralyzing doubt in their own capabilities, people may settle for a job where they simply go through the motions but don't feel fulfilled or inspired.

Finding a job that keeps you interested and engaged will naturally ensure that you stay motivated. If you are constantly battling boredom and frustration, you will have a much harder time completing tasks. The ideal job should be an amalgam of what you are good at, what you enjoy doing, and what someone will pay you to do.

There are many occupational paths that people with ADHD excel at, like jobs that are more creative than analytical/logistical (designer versus tailor; advertising/marketing versus accounting/money management, inventor versus engineer). Don't get me wrong; you can pursue any career you like. It is just that finding a more natural fit generally ensures longevity. This is part of the reason I am better suited to be a psychiatrist versus a surgeon.

Other job modalities that generally have good outcomes are ones that permit flexibility for ADHD nuances. Working for yourself tends to be successful because you run by your own deadlines and supervision, you can take time away without inconveniencing others, and you flourish creatively in random bursts of hyperfocus. You can work at your own pace and may be more stimulated by environments that are constantly changing. One of your strengths may be your finely honed social skills. If this is the case, you may do extremely well in a career that is heavy on customer interfacing or public-serving efforts.

It is equally important to know which careers may potentially be restrictive for you. Jobs that don't engage you, that involve mountains of reading or paperwork, or that are socially isolating may not suit you.

Finding the right fit is a labor of love. Dedicate some time and truly think about a job that could make you happy on a long-term basis. Talk to other people in the field and get first-hand knowledge of the inner workings of the interview process. You can even ask to shadow someone currently in that position to see what the day-to-day flow would be like.

Do you feel like you are in a career that (truly) fulfills you?

Embrace Challenges

We often believe that since we have ADHD, we are destined to fail at things that other people find challenging. This mindset often prevents us from even attempting these endeavors and can limit our options and growth. The truth is that our unique neurobiology might actually make us *better* suited to handle certain challenges. In embracing our differences and focusing on our positive attributes, we can and *should* charge forward bravely in areas where others have stumbled.

Gaining the confidence to boldly face challenges starts with accepting your ADHD. As you understand more about your inner workings, you can start to live your life more aligned with your capabilities. Everyone with ADHD has different challenges and assets, so become an expert on your own ADHD.

You also must reassess years of negative input. You must heal the low self-esteem caused by harsh criticism. You must acknowledge and face the fear of failure. You must start to use your own internal metrics rather than comparing your brain to neurotypical brains because, on the most fundamental level, *they are different.*

You can embrace these challenges in two ways. One is to accept your ADHD and find a strategy that caters to your neurobiology to address it. The second is to recognize that this is an area you struggle with and to remove the shame and guilt associated with it (which makes you less scared to fail).

Compensate for Poor Memory

Having a poor memory is not anything new to people with ADHD. With a brain that goes a million miles an hour, it is so hard to effectively process and categorize all that data, much less retrieve it on demand. This can be especially problematic if you are working in a team setting, frustrating for management if you cannot adhere to deadlines, and personally discouraging to not be able to produce work that you know you are capable of. Here are some suggestions to easily enhance your memory:

- Take notes. If someone tells you something, ask them to summarize it in an email. If someone leaves you a voicemail, replay it while you write down important details.

- Make to-do lists. Break down tasks into doable chunks so that you can use contextual clues to predict what is next.

- Arrange your visual space. Use this as a way of visually reminding yourself what to do. Organize your desk with places to store your papers based on priority. Have a white board with reminders. Utilize your computer to give yourself visual notices when you open your laptop.

- Sync your technology. Part of the battle in this increasingly digital world is that we have ten thousand places to store data. *Sync All of Them.* And when you have a date or deadline to remember, put it where it needs to go immediately; don't assume you will remember to do it later (because you won't; we both know that).

Manage Time Blindness

Have you ever gotten so engrossed in something and then look at the clock and are shocked to see it's been hours when you thought minutes have gone by? My favorite quote on this topic is by Dr. Russell Barkley, who said that ADHD disrupts the fabric of time.

This is a major source of frustration for people who do not experience this phenomenon. "You do the same thing every day, so why are you always late?" "Why did you start doing that knowing you had to be there in five minutes?" "You own a watch, so why don't you look at it?" My response to every neurotypical judgmental comment is "My time works differently than yours."

The ability to gauge the passing of time is one facet of executive function and is more complicated than it first seems. To have a good sense of time, you need to know what time it is currently, how much time is left, and how quickly time is elapsing. People with ADHD have a very weak concept of all of those. So how do you manage this unique and disabling phenomenon?

- **Be aware of things that can cause you to "lose" time.** There are certain tasks or topics that you can get lost in. Generally, they are things that you are naturally interested or engaged in or something repetitive that you are getting some pleasure out of accomplishing. Either way, recognize what those things are and avoid them if you are in a time crunch, or safeguard yourself with external reminders to help you stop.

- **Utilize alarms.** Alarms are a simple, effective tool to increase your awareness of time. They can pierce through hyperfocus and act as an external milepost to assess time progression. Don't be afraid to set as many alarms as you need, but make sure you alternate and change your alarm sounds; otherwise, you are just going to ignore them.

- **Build in buffer periods.** Building in that breathing room or scheduling specific free periods of your day can prevent you from being stifled by your own schedule and may help stave off being overwhelmed. Even if you fall off track, those blank periods can help you course-correct (even a scheduled fifteen-minute break in the afternoon when your energy starts to dip could be enough to de-escalate your day).

By analyzing your understanding of time and figuring out potential pitfalls and solutions ahead of time, you have a better chance of overcoming time blindness.

Manage Procrastination

Procrastination is a common phenomenon with ADHD. Due to difficulties with executive functioning, it is often hard for people with ADHD to figure out the steps needed to complete a task. This can explain why it is easier to delay things than take the cognitive toll of figuring it out in the moment.

The issue with procrastination is that it not only prevents the completion of tasks; it can also impact those around you in a professional setting. In your brain, you may have the utmost confidence that things *will* get done (in part because you hope the adrenaline of leaving something to the last minute will propel you to the finish line), but that is not aligned with neurotypical thinking.

So here are some ways to manage the procrastination beast:

- **Set deadlines.** If something is due in a week, plan to be done in four days. If you don't meet the deadline, you have some built-in buffer time.

- **Break down the tasks.** Breaking things into smaller tasks gives you the dopamine rush of getting things done (even if they are small), which puts you in a better mindset to attack bigger items.

- **Have frequent check-ins.** Having someone to hold you accountable (not micromanage!) can help keep you on task and prevent you from pushing things to the end.

- **Reward yourself throughout.** If you associate the task you are trying to complete with positive rewards, you are more likely to continue to motivate yourself forward.

Learn to Delegate

The ADHD brain is already running at maximum capacity, so anything that can take some stress off your plate should be welcomed. Life is so much easier once you learn how and what to delegate.

Many successful people are adept at delegating, but few adults with ADHD have mastered this skill. To know what to hand off to others, you need to be able to plan multiple steps down the road, envision the progress in a multifaceted way, communicate clearly and directly, and be able to set goals that integrate numerous pieces of information.

On top of challenges brought on by poor executive functioning, you must also overcome certain psychological barriers. You may opt to do things yourself because you are ever cognizant of the tired trope "if you farm it out, you are lazy." You may also fall victim to your people-pleasing tendencies or bypass interactions that may incur rejection.

It can be difficult to sort out what to delegate, to whom, and how to do it. Here are a few tips so you can start reassigning some of that workload: Be clear about how you want things done. It may even be helpful to record an example of what you want done so that it is easier to execute your vision. Explain why you need this help in a way that mutually benefits both parties (phrase your request as a shared goal so it doesn't feel like you are dumping work on others).

Learn to Prioritize

Prioritizing is a unique concept. It is the ability to determine the order for dealing with a series of items or tasks according to their relative importance. Neurotypical brains automatically sort things into a list of items in descending order of importance. My brain does *not* do that. If I somehow manage to get a to-do list together, I usually find a way to work through the easier ones first, which keeps me busy, but I'm not necessarily making progress. I know what I need to do, but I can't figure out how to initiate something complex, so I keep occupied with easier but less critical tasks. What's even more infuriating is that tasks that have never been on my radar because they are so low on the scale of priorities now seem more appealing in comparison to higher-priority items. (So now I am suddenly cleaning the grout in the shower instead of doing my way-more-imminent taxes? Why brain? Why?)

So how do you prioritize if your brain is simply not wired in a way to do so? Because adults with ADHD often struggle with executive function and self-regulation, completing tasks can be difficult and large projects can seem daunting. To work past this:

- **Decide what to attempt first based on *importance*.** Ask yourself, what is the most important task that you need to accomplish, and then order your other priorities after that one. Your brain probably wants to do the easy tasks and postpone the "big" things, but at the end of the day if you start with those, you may have an entire checklist of seemingly trivial things accomplished with very little productive progress made.

- **Do things one at a time.** Break down large projects or jobs into smaller, sequential, manageable steps. Instead of saying something like "Write chapter of self-care book," break it down into "Walk upstairs to laptop," followed by "Get out reference texts," then "Pull up relevant tabs," and so forth until you get to "Write." If you want a more detailed rant on multitasking, head to the "Do One Thing at a Time" entry in Chapter 6.

- **Stay on task.** Avoid getting sidetracked by sticking to your schedule and using a visual timer to enforce it. The other key here is to reframe your understanding of time. For example, if one hour seems like mentally way too long of a time, you can tell yourself to work on your task until the end of the soundtrack you're listening to (the *Garden State* soundtrack is 52:55, in case you were curious).

As with other entries, prioritizing isn't something that is going to happen overnight. There are a lot of small steps while you are learning to prioritize that can help you optimize efficiency and effectiveness.

Counteract Restlessness

Fidgeting and restlessness are real problems, especially among people with the hyperactive presentation of ADHD. People self-select into careers that permit lots of movement (sales, culinary services, and even certain specialties in medicine like emergency medicine). But sometimes we are chained to our desks. We recognize that as adults we can't be constantly running around and squirming through meetings, so here are some ways to counteract restlessness in a professional setting:

- **Take breaks.** Taking intermittent breaks to walk to get water or to the bathroom or check your mail all serve to stretch your legs and prevent that overwhelming sensation of being agitated in your seat.

- **Take walks.** If you can take a break, get some exercise. Use the stairs instead of the elevator, walk outside during lunch, and just move around to enhance your circulation.

- **Take notes.** If the thought of a long meeting already gets you writhing, think about taking notes. It occupies you physically and distracts the rest of your body. As a bonus, it keeps you more engaged in the topic!

- **Become creative in movement.** Stuck at a desk? Think about a standing desk or an under-the-desk bike pedal exerciser or even just doing a few yoga poses and stretching.

Arrange Your Workspace for Reward

Having a spot to work that uniquely suits your neurodivergent brain can make a huge difference in terms of your ability to focus and complete tasks. Here are a couple of tips to make your workspace into a space that works:

- **Prioritize comfort.** ADHD brains will fixate on any extraneous stimuli, so if something is making you uncomfortable, that's going to become your primary focus. Find furniture that you wouldn't mind spending a significant portion of your day in and around. Find the right height and placement for your computer/monitor. Find an ergonomic keyboard and mouse system (wireless options give a lot of flexibility).

- **Minimize clutter.** Although you probably know where everything is despite the outward mess, clutter eventually becomes overwhelming and impacts productivity. Try using a filing system by priority. Also, keeping your desk as clear as possible is best for keeping order. Move any papers that are not urgent to a nearby drawer; they don't need to be cluttering up your desk.

- **Make it interesting.** Your brain works best when it is stimulated and engaged. Unfortunately, work can sometimes be tedious and boring. Do your more menial tasks alongside a stimulating playlist (if that is feasible) or with the use of small rewards ("If I get this done by 4 p.m., I can walk downstairs for a snack").

If you have a job that allows latitude in creating a workspace that will optimize your professional performance, find the configuration that works for you!

Learn to Manage Long-Term Projects

The ADHD brain is not wired to think in the long term. It wants to deal with what is happening right *now*. That is part of the reason we have such a hard time planning something in the future. We have difficulty managing complex, long-term projects because of our poor executive functioning. Here are some tips to help us tackle these long-term challenges:

- **Break things into manageable parts.** It requires skill to disassemble a project into practical pieces so you can figure out the order you want to tackle them. Try to look at the big picture and figure out what it would take to get from start to finish. Once you have a rough order of how to complete the ask, create a timeline and try to complete each portion before its deadline so you build in a buffer in case procrastination and distraction decide to visit.

- **Work with someone on the organizational front.** Recognize that organizing may not be your strong suit and utilize someone else's brain to accomplish the "nitty gritty" details. By delegating some things early in the process, you may build a framework that is easy to sustain for the long haul. You will learn to utilize your strengths and, more importantly, offset your weaknesses to help you accomplish projects more efficiently.

- **Be realistic about your goals.** Work to find reasonable timelines while factoring effort, timing, and potential for burnout. If you have the opportunity for a more leisurely pace, take it.

- **Reward yourself.** Filling up that dopamine bucket as you progress ensures continued motivation, which will gas up your tank for the next part of the journey.

CHAPTER SIX

Practical Self-Care

The ADHD brain views structure as a paradox: You hate feeling limited and confined, but you need some structure to succeed. This is part of the reason it is so vital to find a routine or structure to simplify your life and regain some calmness and control. Practical self-care refers to the actions you take to fulfill your core needs and decrease stress.

Most neurodivergent people may have difficulty pinpointing when they last felt "in control" of things. Due to our brains whizzing at incredible speeds, it is so easy to forget details, make careless mistakes, or veer from routine. Often your best intentions can be foiled by your lack of preparation, difficulty maintaining focus, or poor time management. Your best chance for keeping your life in order (and your head above water) is to learn and utilize methods that help with your day-to-day functioning.

Activities in this chapter include learning how to budget, dealing with messes, and minimizing distraction. Perhaps these are not the most exciting forms of self-care, but they are important. Having these fundamental processes aligned for efficiency (and not just on the precipice of chaos) frees up a great deal of mental energy to spend on things you enjoy.

Understand Your Diagnosis

ADHD is a neurodevelopmental disorder that manifests as a pattern of inattention, hyperactivity, or a combination of both. The symptoms can interfere significantly with your daily activities and relationships and are *not* just limited to focus. ADHD begins in childhood and can continue into adulthood.

Many adults with ADHD don't even know that they have it. The level of awareness about this neurological diagnosis has increased in recent years, but previously it has been overlooked or misdiagnosed as a mood or behavioral issue. Diagnosis may also have been delayed or skipped in part due to people camouflaging symptoms to appear less impaired. However, as life becomes increasingly more complex and demanding, it is often difficult to mask your symptoms effectively, and you will start seeing serious deficits come to the surface.

The concept of getting "labeled" with a diagnosis can either be a deterrent to getting help or result in a sigh of relief that there is a name and explanation for your constellation of symptoms. Here are some things a formal diagnosis can provide:

- Validation of previous life choices
- Direction for behavioral modification
- Potential for medication
- Possible accommodations at school or work

Perhaps the best reason, to me, is to understand your brain better. I know access to care isn't always available, but educating yourself is often the best first step.

Find the Right Doctor

Working with a mental health professional should be a collaborative experience because, unlike looking at scans or lab values or broken bones, a vast majority of diagnostic data comes from what the patient shares about their internal experience. It can feel very intimate because you are discussing things that you may consider private. You are also placing a great deal of trust and faith in the provider that they understand what you are relaying and that they can work with you to come to a solution.

So how do you find the "one"?

- Get referrals. You can get this information from many sources: your insurance, your primary care doctor, your friends/family, or even social media.

- Review credentials. Factor in if the doctor has had specialized psychiatry training and what their areas of expertise are.

- Know what is important to you in a provider. For example, gender, age, if they do certain procedures, and so on.

- Look at reviews. Even great providers can have intermittent bad reviews, but if you are seeing a pervasive pattern, you should go elsewhere.

- Assess communication style. When meeting with the doctor, assess if you feel comfortable, heard, and understood. See if they are approaching things collaboratively. Assess if it's a good fit!

Having difficulty knowing who is who in terms of mental health-care? Head to the next entry for a cheat sheet!

Learn the Different Players
of Your Care Team

Figuring out what is available to you is one thing, but figuring out the distinctions between different levels of training can be confusing. Here's a little cheat sheet.

- **Psychiatrists.** Psychiatrists are physicians that have gone through medical school (MD or DO) and have completed psychiatric training. They can diagnose mental health conditions, prescribe and monitor medications, and provide therapy. Some have completed additional specialty training.

- **Primary Care Physicians.** Primary care physicians and pediatricians (MD or DO) can prescribe medication, but you might first consider someone who specializes in mental healthcare for a diagnosis if you/ they feel more comfortable with that course of action. Primary care and mental health professionals can work together to determine an individual's best treatment plan.

- **Psychiatric Nurse Practitioners.** Psychiatric nurse practitioners (PMHNP) can provide assessment, diagnosis, and therapy for mental health conditions. In some states, they are also qualified to prescribe and monitor medications but may require supervision by a licensed psychiatrist.

- **Family Nurse Practitioners.** Family nurse practitioners (FNP) can provide general medical services and can prescribe medication but may not specialize in mental healthcare. They may also be under supervision by a licensed physician depending on the state.

- **Psychiatric Pharmacists.** Psychiatric pharmacists are pharmacists who specialize in mental healthcare. They can prescribe or recommend appropriate medications (if allowed in their state and practice setting) and are very well trained in medication management (some duties include making recommendations and describing how to modify treatment, managing medication reactions and drug interactions, and providing pharmacologic education).

- **Psychologists.** Psychologists (PhD or PsyD) hold a doctoral degree in clinical psychology or another specialty such as counseling or education. They can make diagnoses and provide individual and group therapy. Some may have training in specific forms of therapy.

- **Counselors, Clinicians, Therapists.** These masters-level healthcare professionals (LPC, LMFT, MS, or MA) are trained to use therapeutic techniques based on specific training programs.

- **Clinical Social Workers.** Clinical social workers (LCSW, MSW) are trained to evaluate mental health and use therapeutic techniques to aid in treatment. They are also trained in case management and advocacy services.

Although this list is cursory, it includes some basic terminology and helps you make distinctions between levels of care. Understanding each role helps you ascertain what would be a suitable fit. As a psychiatrist, I generally encourage people to find a care team that is tailored to their unique needs. This can change as your journey progresses, but it is vitally important to educate yourself and utilize resources around you (if they are accessible).

Ask for Help

There is no medal if you do everything on your own. It is not a rite of passage to be more miserable than the rest of your peers.

Here is a tip that changed the game for me. If something does not interest you, ask for help. For the more menial, tedious, and time-consuming challenges that take up your time and energy, ask someone else to step in (if that is possible). Perhaps you assumed this behavior was reserved for the exorbitantly wealthy or severely incapacitated? Wrong. It is a brilliant tool to take things off your plate that you simply don't care about.

If my options are to pay a cleaner once a month or feel like I am suffocating in my own disaster, it is a no-brainer for me. I won't hesitate to hire professional movers instead of personally disassembling, packing, and moving all my furniture. If I feel overwhelmed by drowning in paperwork and cannot stay organized, I will bring in a secretary once a quarter to file and fax and discard things. And when money is the limiting factor, then ask a friend to just be there with you and lend a hand. Having someone else physically or virtually present (head over to the "Find a Body Double" entry in Chapter 5 to see why) makes it easier to complete hideously dull tasks.

Create a Budget

Managing your finances can be difficult because you must plan, be organizationally rigid, and fight against impulsivity all at the same time. Here are three things that just make cents (I know, I am hilarious):

- Track your spending. Having good information about your spending habits is often pivotal in managing your finances. Find a way to track and figure out *what* you spend money on (this can be made easier by banking apps). If you do this for a month, that's a good sample size of data to use for a realistic budget.

- Figure out your unnecessary/impulse purchases. While you can't always account for these types of purchases, it is good to know what they are so you can budget accordingly. Also, if you know you are going to a place where you typically overspend or impulse buy, bring cash so you have a firm limit on what you are able to spend.

- Use technology to assist you with money management. Tracking your finances, paying bills online to avoid late fees, and providing resources to help you manage financial endeavors more efficiently are just a few of the ways online banking platforms can help you. It may be annoying to set up an account, but in the long run, this will make your life significantly easier.

As an honorable mention: Unsubscribe from shopping emails!

Do One Thing at a Time

Spoiler alert: I don't think anyone can effectively "multitask." I think rather than actually doing two or three tasks simultaneously, you are just switching from one task to another (your brain is simply processing one task at a time). A study out of Stanford showed that chronic multitasking makes you *less* effective at work and impacts your ability to make decisions. For ADHD brains that claim that they are good at multitasking, I ask you this: "Are you really good at multitasking, or do you just have a lot of energy to be able to do many things (but not necessarily do them well or to completion)?"

Having many transitions as you move between tasks may cause you to lose track of where you were, make careless mistakes, require more time to complete something, or even potentially spiral into feeling exhausted and overburdened. The Stanford study found that chronic multitasking was a vicious cycle. The more people are interrupted (especially by engaging dopamine-rich surges!), the shorter their attention spans become. These disruptions give just enough stimulation that you start to *create* your own interruptions (taking a break to check your *Instagram*, sending a text to start a conversation, and so on), which pull you further from completing your tasks. ADHD brains are already wired to poorly regulate interruptions, so this further exacerbates your ADHD symptoms.

Society is shifting to an unconscious standard of doing lots of things at once. We live in an era when we cannot even go to the bathroom without mindlessly scrolling through our phones. In fact, being chronically overloaded with tasks and doing numerous things at once now translate to carrying importance in society. We are all coveting an unsustainable model. So how do you dial down to do one thing at a time?

- **Prioritize.** It is important to know what needs to get done first so that your attention doesn't get pulled by more extraneous tasks. Ideally, if you can sort your list by importance, you can make progress, and as your focus wanes and your tendency to succumb to distractions increases, you may be further down your to-do list.

- **Break down tasks into manageable chunks.** The ADHD brain really likes making *progress*. If you break something down into smaller chunks that are easily achievable, you may feel validation that you are moving forward, which in turn motivates you to keep going.

- **Minimize distractions.** Hide your phone or put it on "do not disturb." Put limitations on usage of social media. Block certain sites while you are working. You're the most likely culprit when it comes to distracting yourself.

Do What You Are Doing Now

I constantly want to do all the things at once. I often start things with high energy and endless aspirations, but I soon find it hard to stay on task or get projects finished. The stress we experience doesn't come from having too much to do. It stems from not finishing what we've started.

When things get difficult or boring, the ADHD brain loses steam, and loses steam quickly. That deceleration encourages us to switch tasks in an effort to be more productive. Maybe if we can tick something off our to-do list, *that* might give us the motivation to keep going? In reality, it just leads us to numerous half-finished projects.

How can you fix this? Do what you are doing now. If you have started a project, try to stay on that task because, in the end, that is what is going to simplify your to-do list and lead to more tasks being completed successfully. Instead of jumping around with a little of this and a little of that, muscle through the more cognitively demanding task (because it will not be easier if you procrastinate or forget about it entirely).

When you feel that urge to jump ship and complete the easier/more interesting task, just say, "This is what I am doing now." Say it out loud. It works almost like an external motivation and strengthens your resolve to get that thing done.

Change Your Venue

Due to your unique operating system, you're better off trying to work with your brain instead of against it. When you find it difficult to stay dialed in to something, it may be easier to change external factors rather than attempt to wrestle your brain into submission.

Sometimes you need a reset for your brain to get a fresh start to focus on things. One of the easiest ways to do that is to change your venue. Many of us have consistently been told to place a premium on routine, but breaking those routines can sometimes allow us to access novel ideas and innovations.

When you change your routine, you are exposing yourself to new stimuli and can start to alter your perception. Something as simple as changing your location can interrupt your patterns and reignite your brain. Typically, when I fall into a stagnant pattern, I take that as a sign to pack up and go somewhere else: coffee shop, open green space, or even just a different place in my house (I am currently writing this chapter from an empty bathtub!).

If you don't have a lot of flexibility in terms of physical location, just change where you put your computer, or tweak the placement of your chair, or try to stand instead of sit. The idea is to jump-start your brain into thinking it is in a new location, so it starts to approach things with a fresh, new perspective.

Start Meal Planning

We all recognize the correlation between eating well and better over-all mental health. The problem for people with ADHD is the steps leading up to preparing a meal. The executive planning that goes into decision-making, prioritizing, and the time-management aspect of meal planning makes this a cumbersome chore and is probably part of the reason we make poor food choices.

Planning your meals for the week and making a grocery list require a significant amount of executive-functioning skills. If you already have a poor grasp of this, meal planning can be extremely overwhelming and more work than the benefit it affords. However, incorporating small adjustments and learning this specific skill set can make this a much more tenable process.

First, why should you meal plan? People generally fixate on the fact that it will save you time and money, but I think for people with ADHD, it takes away the element of surprise. Meal planning can eradicate the overwhelm around planning for meals and mitigate the urge to "take the easy way out" and skip a meal or swing by the drive-thru.

The following tips can make this process easier:

- **Set aside time to prepare.** Planning shouldn't be a long process. Write it down somewhere and don't spend the effort memorizing it.

- **Keep a list of recipes** that are quick, easy, and you know how to make (put those on your phone).

- **Plan all your meals.** When you skip planning one meal, it is easy to derail the whole process.

- **Meal prep with a schedule in mind.** On days when you work late, do something easy like putting food in a slow cooker in the morning.

- **Be creative with your leftovers.** You can use them as a repeat meal (less prep and planning!) or freeze portions to eat later. You can also repurpose a base ingredient to be the star in different meals: tacos, salad toppings, soups, and casseroles.

One thing that makes meal planning a little more sustainable is knowing that if you need a break, that's fine too. Not everything in your life has to be rigid and regimented. You can still enjoy restaurants, still follow cravings, and still explore new cuisines when the mood strikes. The purpose of meal planning is to take some of the stress away from the grind of day-to-day planning, not to force you into a monotonous and joyless routine.

Take Something Off Your To-Do List

Struggling with a never-ending to-do list is not only overwhelming; it is also slightly counterproductive. People become so fixated and meticulous about curating this endless list that very little work actually gets accomplished. You may stare at the list and feel overwhelmed by the sheer volume of items, or have them poorly prioritized and spend your time inefficiently. The result is the same: exhaustion, guilt, and lack of productivity.

What if the answer was to take stuff *off* your list? The secret to doing better work and feeling motivated and competent is to do *less*.

That sounds ludicrous, but let me tell you why this is so vital and such an essential form of self-care. You need to do a better job of curating your tasks and discerning what is important enough to utilize your precious attention and what can be delayed or removed from the list. This allows you to streamline your process and gives you greater chances of completion. You can also use the downtime between projects to therapeutically decompress before embarking on your next venture, rather than utilizing all your resources on an activity that didn't need to be done immediately.

This suggestion might be one that anyone would benefit from, but people with ADHD should especially take advantage of this. Learning how to simplify your to-do list will minimize the feeling of being crushed by your obligations and will help you be more productive overall.

Keep Your ADHD in Mind
While Traveling

There is a certain gene mutation (in the gene responsible for dopamine levels) believed to be responsible for restless behavior. This variant makes people more likely to take risks, like packing up and traveling impulsively. When this restless gene is present in children, they are often diagnosed with ADHD.

While the ADHD brain may be predisposed to wanderlust, the actual execution of traveling may be difficult. It can be difficult to coordinate tickets; account for time change; or, the most banal of all, pack for the trip. I always forget something or pack everything I own.

Here are some tips so you can arrive at any destination with your important items:

- Make a checklist. Start making a list two to three days before you start packing. Use the notes app on your phone and keep adding to the list as you remember stuff. By the time you are ready to pack, you should have a fairly comprehensive list.

- Plan your full outfits. Try to envision the trip and what you might be wearing. Say to yourself, "On Friday, I'll wear these pants, this shirt, and these shoes to dinner" instead of "I really like this shirt, I should take it."

- Leave a little room. Your bag should comfortably close and leave some space in case you pick up a few extra treasures or if you're over having to fold things neatly when you leave. It's a welcome change from exceeding the weight limit.

Manage Impulsivity

Impulsivity is not just being rude or a lack of self-discipline. Impulse control is a function of the signaling system of the brain. The part of your brain that controls inhibition (what *stops* you from certain behavior) is called the thalamus. The frontal cortex is the rational part of your brain that deals with processing emotions and problem-solving. The connection and signaling capacity between the two areas is weak in ADHD brains.

That can be the perfect storm for poor judgment and an inability to think about consequences. So often people have asked me, "Why did you do that? Didn't you think about what would happen?" I can honestly say that I hadn't.

What does impulsive behavior look like in ADHD? It often looks like an unpredictable course of action that's based on emotions and not logic. These impulsive behaviors and actions may directly contradict your own plans, habits, and, on occasion, morals and ethics. Many people can be impulsive on occasion, but people with ADHD have such a dysregulation of impulse control that these behaviors can be persistent and span across numerous situations.

Let's break down some things you can do to identify and manage this impulsivity:

- **Become aware of how your impulsivity manifests.** What do you do? When and where are you the most impulsive? What was the consequence of the behavior? By asking yourself questions, you can start to tease apart these behaviors and find underlying trends and patterns so you can better mitigate the factors surrounding them.

- **Mindfulness.** This involves observing the emotional state that may have contributed to the impulsive behavior. Occasionally, being mindful helps to name the "urge" so you can understand what led you to act impulsively (for example, "I feel jealous, which is *why* I want to comment on her photo"). Once you can recognize things that preempt those impulsive urges, you can slow down enough to think about what the next steps are.

- **Prepare ahead of time and sabotage your own impulsivity.** Once you recognize what you do and why you do it, then you literally must be smarter than your brain. Overspend? Pack cash for a shopping trip and leave your card at home. Overeat? Put chips in a bowl instead of bringing the entire bag over to the couch. Overshare? Bring a notepad and write down your thoughts rather than blurting them out because you are worried you will forget them.

It seems like a paradox to try to control impulsivity, but you can practice and potentially bypass a lot of grief by utilizing these techniques. With appropriate therapy, behavioral modification, and medication (if appropriate), you can slow things down and train your brain to *think* before you *do.*

Prevent Distracted Driving

Adults with ADHD struggle with inattentiveness and distractibility at our baseline, so we need to be aware of how that may present while driving, not only for ourselves but also for the safety of others. People with ADHD are at greater risk for traffic-related accidents, receiving speeding/parking tickets, and emotional dysregulation while driving (road rage!).

Due to limitations in executive functioning and decreased frontal lobe activation (heightened impulsivity, poor judgment, seeking stimulation by risky behavior), there is an increased probability of negative outcomes while driving. We may be less responsive to other drivers or road conditions, yet we have an unwarranted confidence in our driving abilities.

Furthermore, a constant connection to our mobile devices means that we are traveling with something that will take our eyes off the road. Phones aren't the only distraction: People in the car, children in the back seat, changing the radio station, eating, drinking, adjusting your makeup can all lead to negative outcomes. We are especially at risk when the drive is under-stimulating. Our brains are desperate to find a way to occupy that time and space, so there is a much higher risk of distracted driving.

Understanding how your ADHD symptoms affect your driving can help you make better safety decisions. Depending on your deficits, you may need to address how to improve reaction times and your ability to sustain focus while driving or how to manage emotional dysregulation.

One of the most helpful things you can do to improve outcomes is to minimize distractions!

Make Your Bed

I fully recognize how dumb this sounds, but it is a game changer. This might be one of the first self-care tidbits I started to employ on my ADHD journey, and I didn't even know why I was prioritizing it. It just made me feel *better*.

This is not just a habit for the obsessively fastidious. The rest of my house can be an utter disaster, but my bed *will be made*. The routine and ritual of making my bed start my day off with a win. I have already checked off my first box of the day, and, honestly, that teeny, little dopamine rush compels me to continue that forward momentum. As I flap out sheets and karate chop pillows, I am taking some time to breathe and mindlessly organize what is going to happen next. Just the physical act of making the bed is strangely calming and therapeutic.

But that is not the only benefit. In medical school, I found that if my bed was made, I was less likely to climb back into it when I felt low on energy or defeated. When I walked into my room with a made bed, I felt more organized and ready to tackle other challenges. I also found that it made getting back into bed at night feel like a luxury. Instead of an unkempt mess of sheets, I'd be turning down the covers as if I was at a hotel.

Try it for a week. See if you notice a difference.

Deal with the Mess!

I am messy. There, I said it. My brain doesn't even register the mess, and I can walk right past it because my whole life is crumpled piles, overflowing baskets, and chaotic drawers filled with tangled cords. WHY ARE WE LIKE THIS? Due to issues with executive functioning, we can start projects but not finish them, have difficulty maintaining routine and consistency, and intrinsically lack motivation to do something boring like cleaning. This is all tolerable UNTIL the mess gets overwhelming and suddenly you look around and feel hopelessly lost. It may seem impossible to climb out of this discarded-sweatshirt-lined hole you've created.

We all know that to keep things tidy and organized, you need to deal with your current mess first. Here are some very tangible, judgment-free ways to do that:

- **Pick up thirteen things.** One of the hardest things about cleaning is knowing where to begin. That's the great thing about this little hack. You're just counting and picking up. Doesn't matter where you start or what you grab: Just pick up thirteen things that are out of place. Eventually, something in your brain is going to catch up to your behavior and trigger a cascade of positive reinforcement to help you keep going.

- **Make piles.** I usually do "trash," "clothes," and "other." If it's out of place, put it in a pile.

- **Play music.** Playing music helps you become and stay engaged in the task *and* can prevent time blindness (see the "Manage Time Blindness" entry in Chapter 5), as you are internally gauging your progress by when the song is ending.

- **Get help.** Get your friends, spouse, or parent to help you with this process. And for the exceptionally out-of-control mess, *hire* someone if possible. You don't need a 24/7 cleaning crew, but hiring a one-time (or once a month) professional can make a huge difference. There have been times when I would have happily spent half my paycheck to achieve a livable space again.

- **Throw it away.** I'm not kidding. I get that this sounds wasteful and exorbitant, but people with ADHD have a hard time assigning value to things. They may have emotional ties to clothes that don't fit or refuse to part ways with a cookie pan that is unusable because of all the oily buildup on it. Donate it if it is in decent shape, recycle it if you can, and if you just need it *out* of there for your own sanity, get rid of it.

Brain Dump Before Bed

There is always so much in my brain that it is impossible to organize it in a meaningful way in real time. As a result, I often forget things amid that neural clutter. It seems that my brain is the busiest at the times when it is supposed to be quieting down. I come up with *great* ideas at bedtime and want to execute them right away, but the rational side of my brain knows I need sleep.

Enter the brain dump.

Write down any to-do items/thoughts you may need later. Spilling all those unfiltered, unprocessed thoughts into one spot gives you raw data that you can sort through at a more appropriate time.

- Break items down. Break a big project ("write book") into smaller tasks that you could reasonably do ("find charger for laptop," "write three more table of contents items," or "proofread introduction"). This makes the bigger project feel more manageable and prevents you from getting overwhelmed.

- Make tasks actionable. Start with a verb and tell yourself to do something. For example, "take medication at 6 a.m." instead of "medication."

- Find a way to organize. This can be by priority or by grouping similar items. I generally take another pass at my brain dump and find a way to make sense of it, so I have a clearer place to start the next time I look at it. By the end of the process, I have a rough to-do list and a running list of ideas that I don't want to forget (that's usually where my more creative ideas go!).

Focus On Progress and Not Results

Most people are trained to think that their success is measured by the outcome. If they didn't reach *that* goal, then they failed. That is so one-dimensional!

When you start focusing your energy more on the processes and the techniques involved and less on the results, you have a higher likelihood of success and greater satisfaction with the outcome. Here are some of the reasons why you need to shift your mindset:

- **You have more satisfaction in the journey.** By staying present in the process, you can enjoy it more fully. This helps the ADHD brain remain engaged and continues to propel you forward.

- **You cope with mistakes better.** Instead of mistakes derailing you, you use them to learn, grow, and adapt. By fixating less on the outcome, you take risks that may help you reach your goals more effectively.

- **You can reduce distractions.** Focusing on the process helps eliminate the "noise" of external factors. You remove some of that additional pressure and anxiety that cloud your executive functioning.

- **You gain autonomy.** Instead of making your happiness contingent on attaining a particular result, let your bliss be driven by the amount of effort you put into the process and how much you have learned on the way. With this simple shift, you gain ownership of the process.

Shut Out Distraction

The concept of focusing implies that you can tune out extraneous and frivolous input and dial in to what you are presently attending to. People with ADHD have an ineffective filter for external stimuli and so are especially prone to distraction. Distractibility does not necessarily mean that you can't focus but rather that you focus on too many things at once.

You can get distracted by visual stimuli: You walk to the other room to get the remote and end up cleaning the microwave. You can get distracted by auditory stimuli: You are trying to take a test but fixating on someone's tapping foot. You can get distracted by tactile stimuli: You are in conversation but becoming preoccupied with an itchy shirt tag. You can even get distracted by your own thoughts!

What does this internal distractibility look like? Jumping from one tangential thought to another. A sea of thoughts all fighting for primary attention. Difficulty engaging in conversation because you may be off topic or "zoning out." I have told people that living in my brain can sometimes feel like a radio scanning through stations. I have these loud, fleeting thoughts that whiz by so quickly it is often difficult to hold on long enough to figure out the song.

Struggling with internal distractibility is burdensome. It can be overwhelming to you and exasperating for your surrounding circle. But learning about your brain is powerful. You can learn to behaviorally manage that inner interference and hopefully cement neural pathways so that distractibility becomes less of a chronic hindrance.

Here are five tips to help cope with distractions:

- **Vocalize boundaries.** Let people know when you need to focus and ensure you create the opportunity to have some uninterrupted, quiet, distraction-free time.

- **Visualize the steps.** Picture the steps required to finish the task at hand. Ask yourself questions as you attempt to break down the task into smaller pieces: What do I need to do next? When should I be done with this? What will it look like when it is done?

- **Be aware of your emotional climate.** Trying to start a task while disappointed or angry can be so internally distracting that it is almost impossible to truly attend to it.

- **Be positive.** Encourage yourself and utilize proof of what you have already accomplished to provide yourself with some dopamine to override other stimulating distractions and keep going.

- **Find an accountability partner.** Share goals and timelines with someone who can keep you on task and partake in the celebrations of hitting your goals!

Start Habit Stacking

A habit is an acquired behavior pattern that is regularly followed and repeated until it can occur almost on autopilot. When a behavior becomes automatic, the ADHD-induced pitfalls (like time blindness, disorganization, or unnecessary distraction) cease to impact you.

So how do you build a habit?

- **Figure out what your current habits are.** Some habits are ingrained into your routine, but maybe they aren't making your life easier. Maybe they aren't worth the stress or financial burden. Can they be improved or replaced with something else?

- **Start stacking.** Start building a new habit by attaching it to an already established habit. That way, you are more likely to maintain the behavior.

- **Celebrate your progress.** We're all about the dopamine rush, right? To motivate sustained effort, log your progress in an app, buy yourself a coffee, or do something positive to encourage momentum. (For more on *why* you should celebrate those small wins, flip to the "Celebrate Your Small Wins" entry in Chapter 1.)

- **Be gentle with yourself.** It is hard to make a habit, and it's even harder when your brain literally wants to do everything in its power to keep things interesting and spontaneous. You're not going to stick to your habit 100 percent of the time. Understand that, and know that you are aiming for forward progress.

Plan Your Day the Night Before

Planning can be a difficult skill set for people with ADHD to master because it requires so many different aspects of executive function. However, with practice, you can start to incorporate planning into your day. Planning helps you become more efficient and effective, and it leaves less to chance. Often when people with ADHD have large windows of unplanned time, they squander that time rather than completing items on their to-do lists. Here are a few tips to help manage your planning so that you can manage your day:

- **Set time aside for planning.** Dedicate a time each day to sit down and plan. Sometimes setting an alarm can help build this into a routine.

- **Decide what is most important.** Prioritizing based on importance is vital, but also try to figure out which task is cognitively the most demanding, and try to knock that out early when you're fresh.

- **Write it down.** Relying on memory is an imperfect system. Put the details in your phone/planner/whatever you use.

- **Be realistic about time goals.** When you are planning for the day ahead, try to break your tasks into manageable chunks to prevent burnout. Work in some flex periods and some fun activities so it doesn't feel too draining.

- **Reflect and review.** Learn what works and what doesn't. Course-correct when planning the next day.

Create a Uniform

Getting dressed can sometimes feel like a Herculean chore. You're barely awake, you have to make decisions regarding social propriety and temperature changes, figure out what textural choices are tolerable that day, and, also, *nothing* is clean. One of the perks of having a uniform is that you don't have to think about those variables.

A uniform doesn't have to be a drab, dreary thing you wear every day. It can be pants that you know are the right length and aren't going to squeeze your stomach in the wrong way. It can be different colors of the same shirt that doesn't have an itchy tag or have to be dry-cleaned. Having a set "look" reflects personal style and can even become a memorable part of your persona (think Steve Jobs's turtleneck or Iris Apfel's glasses!). Having a limited set of combinations of clothing takes some of the brain work out of getting ready in the morning and ensures that you are comfortable, presentable, and confident.

This is not to discourage those who live and breathe sartorialism. If you use fashion to express your creativity and relish in piecing together runway-inspired looks, then this entry isn't for you. This is for the people that wake up and immediately feel deflated at the number of options and circuitous thoughts needed to start their day. The key to successfully managing ADHD is to understand the areas in life that could be simplified. Your closet is one of them.

Learn to Manage Boredom

I hate the hopeless stagnation of being bored and, frankly, do everything in my power to avert it. When I feel this way, I desperately jump to any activity to avoid that void. But maybe I've been doing it wrong?

When you allow your brain to quiet down, you switch into lesser-known neural pathways called the default mode network (DMN). This is a group of distinct areas of the brain that are active when your brain is *not* engaged in a task that requires focus. These parts of your brain are rocking and rolling when you think your brain is at rest.

For neurotypical brains, the task-oriented and default networks are reciprocal: As one works more, the other slows down. For ADHD? The DMN is active while the task-oriented parts of your brain are active, which is another possible explanation for why you are more likely to be sucked away by distraction.

Now that you understand the neurobiology, how does this relate to boredom? When your brain starts to de-escalate and sink into the DMN, you may find ideas you've previously tabled because you couldn't give them the appropriate focus, brilliant gems of creativity that you had to put aside due to time constraints, and even memories that you had forgotten about for years.

The next time you fall into the insufferable lull of boredom, hang out there. It won't take long before that DMN kicks in and presents you with something new and interesting to mull over.

Index

About the Author

Dr. Sasha Hamdani is a board-certified psychiatrist and ADHD clinical specialist. In high school, she founded World Harmony Online, a nonprofit organization serving to create a nonviolent and equitable world with access to technology, healthcare, and education for all. She was then accepted into the six-year accelerated BA/MD program at the University of Missouri–Kansas City, did her psychiatry residency training at the University of Arizona–Phoenix Psychiatry program, and completed her final year of training at Kansas University. She currently has a thriving private practice in Kansas City where she sees patients six years old and up. Dr. Hamdani also has a robust social media following on *Instagram* and TikTok (@thepsychdoctormd), where she breaks down stigmas and provides accessible information about ADHD from the unique perspective of someone who has been both a patient and a provider. Most recently, she was selected to participate in the Healthcare Leaders in Social Media roundtable at the White House and continues to work on efforts regarding the healthcare burnout crisis with the vice president and surgeon general.